UNMITIGATED GAUL
A LIFETIME IN FRANCE

A novel memoir

BY
SUZANNE WHITE

Volume One

LADYFINGERS

A Novel Memoir

DEDICATION

First, I dedicate this volume of Unmitigated Gaul to my dear friends new and old. One is silver. The other gold.

Second, I salute Mark Zuckerberg's Facebook application for providing a virtual place where I discovered the sheer joy of meeting my many thousands of readers one by one up close and personal.

And Thirdly I wish to thank everybody who helped me believe in myself and in this book. All of you: Ian Mathie and Gabi Plumm and Flo Selfman. Barbara Campbell and Claire Davis and Sylvia Ashby and Ronnie Golden and Sandy Keefe, James Hernandez, Betsy Brill, Paul Rest, Stephan Miramon, Josef Schwabl, Mary Hess, Jeffrey Spinner, Pat Sharp, Marlane O'Neill, Elizabeth Pochron, Pat Hanson, Wayne Koppleman, Zoe Fitzgerald Carter, Leslie Keenan and Jesse Kornbluth, Ryan Hoskins, Peter Hoskins, George Hoskins and Nicole Hoskins, Mark Princi and Mimi Princi, Claude Lombard, Dorothy Bray, Jerry Littlefield, Ron Koshes, Pete Gerge, Val Pierotti and many more.

Finally, I must thank all the noble, capable French doctors and nurses who have kept me alive and cheerful since my cancer of 2010: Serge Boyer, Emmanuel Guardiola, Letitia Boyer Roussel, Brigitte Keslair, Phillipe Garcia, Thierry Chalvidan, Christine Bodo, Ariel Uzkuras and a slew ore of sundry medical personnel who comforted me when I was so frightened and in pain.

Vive la France!

PART ONE
BUFFALO, NEW YORK

Buffalo gals won't you come out tonight
Come out tonight come out tonight
Buffalo gals won't you come out tonight
And dance by the light of the moon

PROLOGUE

I n 1943 when I was five, I could not possibly have known that in my lifetime female orgasm would become acceptable — even trendy. Back then, I thought I had invented masturbation. I didn't have a name for it. For me, what is now called masturbation was play. Child's play. Occasionally, I shared my intimate games with my childhood friends. Sexual discovery was part of a kid's life — even back then. I kept my finger exercises hidden from the grownups. Was I ashamed? Yes. I was. But nowadays a woman's orgasm is nothing to be ashamed of. It's a familiar, universal pleasure. In my childhood, all diddlings and the thrills they brought me were secrets. Playing with my privates was just that — private. It took me seventy-seven years to dare to write this all down. To let it out of the closet. To make it real. For me. And for you.

I was never normal. Tall for my age, skinny with mouse-brown hair, smallish feet and a comely rump, I raced through my life as though trying to beat it to the finish line. An excess of spirited abandon thrashed about inside my head, teasing the gray matter fore and aft, port and starboard. My mother often compared me to Pesco, our excitable Airedale puppy.

Willy-nilly, I relied on my passionate nature and ardent desires to hack my way through the jungles of childhood. My unruly exuberance made the rules. The child I was simply followed.

No matter the circumstances, my churning mind kept me in motion, my body alive and my soul in a spin. Wherever I went, there was action. All the time. Everywhere.

CHAPTER ONE

U ntil I was five, my mother insisted I succumb to afternoon naps. It had something to do with being in kindergarten all morning, but more to do with being a pest. Each weekday, immediately after we listened to the noontime radio soap opera *The Romance of Helen Trent*, Elva Hoskins, my pretty Irish-American mother, would tie clumsy pink rubber thumb guards on my little hands, cover my gangly body with my by-now-shredded Bunny Blanket, and lay a loving stroke on my forehead saying, "Don't suck your thumb or the Sandman won't come."

While I was still five and tethered to the daily nap routine, I tossed and turned in my maple twin bed, slamming those clumsy great pink rubber thumb guards back and forth on the pillow until I heard Mommy's old Zenith radio mumbling below. Then, gingerly, I untied the pink rubber thumb guards' laces and tiptoed along the carpet, avoiding the squeaky parts of the floor. I stealthed into my mother's dresser drawers, which smelled of her Russian Leather perfume, and silently absconded with nail polish bottles, eyelash curlers and jars of vanishing cream.

Back in my roost, equipped with these wondrous devices, I found God. Where? Right between my thighs, slightly north of the peepee hole. There lived the dandiest toy of all. Just why it felt so warm and tingly when I crawled back into bed and applied cold bottles, tubes, curlers and fingerly caresses, I did not question.

And back downstairs Elva stood facing a spindly wooden ironing board stacked with rolls of moistened men's shirts and girls' dresses with hard-to-iron puff sleeves and stubborn ruffles. It was the Forties. TV in the average home was still but a glimmer in the eye of the Fifties. Without full-time entertainment, Elva's perpetual ironing chore might have seemed to her like drudgery. But her afternoon ironing stints were accompanied by the serial radio vicissitudes of her favorite soap opera characters.

At one p.m. the *Gal Sunday* announcer asked the listening audience the same question: *"Can Sunday, this orphan girl from a little mining town in the West, find happiness as the wife of a wealthy and titled Englishman?"* My mother was rapt.

When I was five and half, I was over the nap stage and they enrolled me in an all-day kindergarten. That September, although I wasn't quite six, I started the first grade. But in 1944, shortly after my sixth birthday I fell ill and was obliged to stay at home for months at a time. The illness was called staphylococcus. The doctor came every day to inject me with penicillin.

With the staph infection I had to be kept out of school, but I did not necessarily have to stay in bed. I just had to be kept warm. To this end, I was often afforded the luxury of perching on a piece of worn carpet on the low kitchen radiator behind my mother's ironing board. I spent months of afternoons this way, listening to Elva's enchanting radio shows. I thought Our Gal Sunday had slim chances of finding happiness with the wealthy and titled Lord Henry Brinthrope. But I forgot my concerns about Sunday's lopsided marriage when *Ma Perkins* came on. After Ma and her happy brood, there was *Life Can Be Beautiful*, which was followed by *Mary Noble, Backstage Wife, Lorenzo Jones* and his Devoted Wife Belle. Then came just plain *Stella Dallas*. Now it was four p.m. Mommy folded up the rickety ironing board and started preparing dinner.

In those days, my father was a butcher. He had hung a large electric clock in his shop's front display window. He had the clock custom made so it sported words in place of the numbers on its stark white face. The words spelled out Hoskins Quality Meats in black. George Hoskins, my meaty father, had opened his first market in 1932. By the time George Junior had arrived in '34, George Senior was on his way to becoming the Lion of the Buffalo, New York butcher trade. He owned three meat shops. By the time little Sally came along, in 1935, the Lion had been elected president of the Buffalo Retail Meat Dealers' Association.

A few years later, in November '38, my own arrival crowded the Hoskins household. The upper flat over my grandmother Hoskins' lower one was decidedly too small. Nanny Hoskins' sour comments intimidated the gentle Elva, my mother, but she had rarely complained. However, when Nanny called her Black Irish and insisted she be un-baptized Catholic and become Episcopalian, Elva put her dainty size 7 triple A foot down and we moved to Tuscarora Road — a more upscale neighborhood.

Big George stepped up to the plate and bought us a tall, brown-shingled corner house with hedges, white wooden gates and wall-to-wall stair carpeting. Thereafter, we resided in a more suitable section of white working class South Buffalo. We left our rugged old Nanny Hoskins to muddle along alone in her own double house on Trowbridge Street off South Park Avenue.

Now our family of five had more space. But the new house with its ample claw-footed dining room table, sprawling living room and five bedrooms did not buy me much bliss. I was a tiny scrap of a girl who didn't always remember to mind her manners. Big George could not bear my table habits and ostracized me to my room practically every night. He hated the way I ate my Brussels sprouts, leaf by delicate leaf. I dug volcanoes in my mashed potatoes, bit at my nails between mouthfuls, made loud glugging noises when I drank my milk and picked my nose during dessert.

Watching me commit these insults to his upwardly mobile sense of himself and his lifestyle inspired my father to scrutinize my every move as I ate. Almost every night, he would snap, "Susie! Go to your room! And don't come out until you're ready to act like a lady."

These table evictions often gave me a wrenching stomachache. I knew that being banished from the table was not fair. *I didn't do it on purpose,* I would mutter under my breath and skulk slowly up the stairs to my room thinking, *When I grow up I'm going to get the police to make him eat a jillion tons of mashed potatoes in just five minutes with a tiny baby spoon.* I loved my Daddy. But I could not get along with the Lion in him.

Thanks to being so often banished to my room without supper, I adapted to my solitude and, in fact, learned to love exile. Eventually, I would even seek its relief through voluntary acts of civil disobedience. On occasion, I intentionally shoveled stew off the edge of my plate, built deeper gravy craters in my mashed potato mounds, or purposely tipped my milk glass just far enough over to create a soggy wet spot on the white tablecloth.

One time, the Lion smacked my knuckles with the back of his table knife, announcing, "If you don't like it here, you can move downtown to the Statler Hotel. I'll pay your bus fare." By age seven and some, I actually hoped my father would exclude me from meals forever. That way I might spend the rest of my life in bed alone with my fingers and a few odd bottles and tools pinched from my mother's aromatic beauty aids drawer.

In the first grade, when I was still but six, I took up with an older woman. Virginia McCarthy was eight. She lived on Shenandoah Street. Every chance we got, Ginger and I played paper dolls. The Hoskins house was close by at the corner of Tuscarora and Narragansett Streets. South Buffalo was a neighborhood of steel-workers who lived in frame houses with small front porches and napkin-sized front lawns. Along the red brick streets stood tidy, proud rows of two-family homes in which the upstairs rented from the down.

Ginger McCarthy's was a downstairs family with upstairs tenants. Ginger had a brother named Dickie. Dickie was almost eleven and, on principle, hated paper dolls and thought girls were beyond dumb. Peeking in on us one rainy afternoon in Ginger's bedroom as we played house and cut out paper dolls, Dickie whispered, "Betcha don't know what real mommies and daddies do to make babies in the night."

My hand shot up. I knew the answer. "Iknow, Iknow, Iknow!" I cried. "They jump up and down on the bed."

Dickie sniggered. His laughter hurt my feelings and raised some doubts. "You don't know about fucking. You don't know about fucking," Dickie chanted in a shrill gremlin voice.

"All right, Dickie," I said as I flounced up off the floor and plunked myself on Ginger's bed, "what is this fucking stuff?"

Dickie's eyes lit up. He whispered, "Fucking is really dirty."

Ginger now took up a perch next to me on the bed, and said, "I sure hope Mommy doesn't know that you know about this fucking thing."

Dickie squatted on the multicolored throw rug next to the bed and snarled, "You shut up, Ginger McCarthy. You dare tell Mommy 'n I'll bust your teeth down your throat."

Ginger went silent and pale beneath her freckles. Dickie had picked up two paper dolls of opposing sexes, laid the lady face up in her electric-blue tank suit, placed the man on top of her in his briefs, showing but a grayish cardboard backing to the bewildered girls. "It goes just like this," Dickie explained, as he unbuttoned the fly of his corduroy knickers to expose a pink-white angleworm that he now held in his hand. He activated this pink worm with one hand and the male doll's pelvis with the other. "The man takes one of these things and puts it into a hole in the lady. Then he jumps around."

10

Ginger stood up, leaned over, swooped the paper figures from his hand and ran out shrieking, "Maaaaahhhmy Maaaaaahhhmy, Dickie's showing Susie his wiener."

I fled, skittering down the McCarthys' four rubber-matted back steps, my heart pounding. Scared. Not so much of Mrs. McCarthy's wrath, but afraid, after Dickie's disgusting display, that my friend Ginger might never ask me over to play paper dolls again.

What is it about Dickie? I thought. I couldn't figure him out. I slowed my run to a saunter as I neared the big Hoskins house on the corner. No matter how repulsive, it seemed to me that Dickie McCarthy had put his finger on something. Perhaps he had begun to uncover the mystery of the nighttime bumpings I heard coming through the wall from my parents' bedroom.

The next day in the school playground, I made an appointment to meet Dickie McCarthy in the bushes at Cazenovia Park on Saturday morning. Dickie showed up and brought along support forces in the persons of Jerry and Marty Littleford and their close and noto- riously unruly crony, Johnny Banks. Johnny was considered one of the big kids. He was twelve, but only in the fifth grade. As he was so tall, Johnny Banks had to scrunch down in order not to be seen above the clump of bushes in which we were holding our powwow.

It was agreed among us that the boys would show me their things, but I only had to touch them if I wanted to. Dickie informed the other boys, "She only gets to depants herself if she promises not to tell."

I promised. Then each of the boys got out a limp dingdong and held it in his hand as though to pee. Dickie's and Jerry's wee-wees were both dead white dangles and seemed even to recoil in the chilly Buffalo air. Jerry's younger brother, Marty, though he appeared interested when he arrived, had backed out of his part of the deal. "I'd rather watch," he said.

Then it was Johnny Banks' turn to exhibit his doodad. Like the others, it came out of his pants limp, an ivory-pink color. But once removed from his trousers' constriction, the pale, pink, shrimpish blob grew purplish-blue. It looked hard.

Having taken a good, yet incredulous look, I found my own voice right there where I had left it some thirty seconds before. "Put that back!" I commanded. "If you catch cold, your mother will kill you."

"It ain't cold." Johnny leered in my direction. "It's hungry."

"Where do you put the food in?" I asked, peering closer.

Johnny's reply was cut off by little Marty's question. "How come it's all red?"

Jerry spoke up too, "How'd you get it so hard?"

Johnny beamed. "When I'm on the toilet sometimes, I just think about some girl. It's easy. You can do it too."

Dickie McCarthy confessed he had done it once. It just went all stiff on him and when he touched it to make it stop, it squirted all over the place.

"I think that's why fathers stick theirs into mothers. First it's to make a baby. But it feels real good, too." Dickie offered.

I shivered. The mechanics seemed impractical. "I could let you put it on top. But don't stick it in me. Okay?" I lowered my drawers around my ankles, stood up and spread the lips of my hairless privacy. I watched them closely as, one by one, the boys lined up to touch their flesh to mine. Their softness felt warm. Baby butterflies fluttered along my thighs. "It feels pretty nice," I had to admit. Each boy's limp peepee came away from my secret folds stiff and strong. Johnny Banks was last in the queue. As he approached for his turn, a scary shudder went down my spine. "You better not," I protested. "I'm afraid."

I was petrified of Johnny Banks and his lurid bludgeon. He looked far too much like somebody who knew what he was doing.

"I ain't gonna hurt you." Johnny took my arm. My cooperation had been won by the other boys' droopy dangles. But this tall boy with his rigid, purplish weapon was different; I just knew that Johnny Banks was not about to settle for a little playful sledding along the lips of my wee wee. His grip tightened on my wrist.

Looking directly at Dickie, I assumed my haughtiest air and said, "Dickie McCarthy, if you don't make Johnny stop right now I'm gonna tell your mother and Mrs. Littleford and Mrs. Banks and ….. and …" I began to cry, gasping, sobby cries, still threatening through the tears, "…. and my mother and the teacher and my father and the police and everybody at School 67 — even Miss O'Rourke."

Miss O'Rourke was the no-nonsense Irish Catholic school principal of PS 67. If O'Rourke found out, we would all be expelled. The other boys combined forces with Dickie. "Aww leave 'er alone," said Dickie. "Yeah. Lay off," added Jerry. "She's a-scared o' you."

I tugged at my red Lollipop undies, raising them hurriedly — and clumsily — up past my knobby knees and onto my shuddering fanny.

In a wink, Johnny Banks' enormous electric eel went all soggy. His face took over in the purple department. By comparison, Rumpelstiltskin was a prince of self-control. "You don't like me. You let everybody else. You let Dickie and the others do it to you." He stomped and raved.

"Aah, your mother wears army shoes," Jerry told him as he buttoned up his own fly.

"She does not!" yelled Johnny. "She does not!" He stomped. His temper raged at full volume. His longish, black hair swung back and forth over his narrowed lids. His naked peter waved about aimlessly. Suddenly, Johnny Banks appeared quite ridiculous. I found myself smiling.

"And she cuts your hair with a bowl on your head!" interjected Dickie.

Johnny buttoned up the fly on his corduroy knickers, lowered his face to the ground and kicked up a lot of dead leaves and sod. "I already told you," he muttered back at them, "she uses a wastebasket."

I was eight years old, frequently ill and a blissfully sickly child at that. The doctor had diagnosed my first ailment as a staphylococcus infection. Penicillin had its way with that. After that came a bout of scarlet fever and a whopping heart murmur. Lastly, I contracted a rare form of infectious hepatitis which back then was simply called yellow jaundice. For almost two years I stayed home from school, read the Bobbsey Twins books and listened to the radio. My big brother George, whom everybody in the neighborhood called The Rooster, kept me amply supplied with stolen comic books and jelly babies that he nicked from the corner store.

My big sister Sally, whom my father had dubbed The Gypsy because of her increasing penchant for makeup and jewelry, shared my bedroom. But we spoke very little.

Occasionally, when I was on my own, sticking jelly babies inside the lips of my private parts, thoughts crept into my mind from out of nowhere. For example, when I was angry with my father, I noted his imaginary presence among some doctors I had conjured up as I closed the eyelash curler on my labia majora until it hurt.

Of course, in these imaginary scenes, the Lion doctor person was never anything but docile and solicitous of my state of health. He would touch my chest and stick funny things in my ears and ask me to say "Ahhh" when he put giant wooden popsicle sticks in my mouth. Then he would seem to consult with the other nice doctors who were there and slowly dissolve into the background as I pondered more serious considerations, such as which creams among seven or eight undercover bottles and jars I would rub on my already sore membranes before continuing with the game.

I returned to regular school in the fifth grade. I was ten. I had been out of class for so long that the only friend I could count on was Charmaine Cutler, the girl whose parents ran the corner candy store. Charmaine was fat, ill-mannered and dull-witted. Charmaine's parents weren't bad. But they were old. Mrs. Cutler was in fragile health. Mr. Cutler was generous, kind and indulgent. Day in and day out, Charmaine wheedled Popsicles, candies and root beers out of him. Night in, night out, Mrs. Cutler complained of splitting headaches and was forever slouching around in a beige, wooly wrap, opening windows to relieve her sweating.

The first time I visited the Cutlers' narrow three-room flat over the candy store, Mr. Cutler took a shine to me. He liked my smiles, my pleases and thank-yous and how-do-you-dos. In a matter of weeks, he had awarded me more Good & Plentys, Snickers, and Clark bars than I had ever before seen in my tiny life. He felt I was a good influence on Charmaine. "You're a very polite little girl," he told me. "You can stick around." So I was invited on many a weekend excursion and frequently cajoled to stay overnight at the Cutlers'. My family's party manners beginning to rub off on the chubby Charmaine. She occasionally said more than just "Gimme" now and her whinings diminished apace. Even Mrs. Cutler smiled more now that I so often stuck around.

So thrilled was Mr. Cutler by these developments that he converted the attic over the store's upper flat into a playroom. Here, we two girls dressed our dolls, practiced magic tricks, daubed finger paints all over the walls and instituted the practice of our most consuming pastime, which we called YoYo — a code word for Doctor. Occasionally, one or the other Cutler parent would call up the attic stairs, "Charm! Susie! What are you doing?" We girls would cry out in lilting unison, "We're playing YoYo."

YoYo was best played by two or more players. It began by each player taking down her underpants and hiding them under the couch cushion. Then, one or the other would climb up on the Ping-Pong table and bare her pillowy privates. Usually, Charmaine went first.

"Did you let a man put his wee-wee in your hole?" I affected a deep doctor voice.

"Once somebody did it to me," Charmaine admitted, with a squeaky voice she thought sounded like a big lady's.

"Did you like it?" I pried.

"It hurt really a lot. But he gave me some candy," admitted the patient.

"It looks serious. Could be you need an operation, my poor woman," I opined.

"Am I still bleeding? Will I live?" Charmaine answered.

"I will have to put my wiener inside you to check. Maybe something got stuck up there. Or maybe it chewed off your stomach," I would say. Placing the neck of an empty Coke bottle against Charm's crotch, I laid the top inside my playmate's lips and moved it around until Charm squealed and said, "That hurts."

Then it was my turn to be the patient. Charm hopped down and I assumed the proper position.

Since Charmaine was not gifted at inventing dialogue, I had written a special YoYo script for her. Uncrumpling the lined notebook paper now, Charm began to read, ponderously, as though from a primer, "How many times did you huck this week, missus?"

I sighed, swiped the paper from Charm's hand and pointed to a word. "That doesn't say huck. I told you already. It's F-U-C-K. Do you see any H in that word?" Resuming my pose, I spread the folds of my coosie and answered the doctor's question: "I think I fucked twenty times this week."

"You got a lotta blood here," said Charm in an affected basso profundo.

15

I writhed. "Now ask me what it felt like. Go on."

"What does it feel like?" Charm said then.

"Not just what does it feel like? That's boring. Read it from the paper, silly. It says more." Charm so exasperated me.

"How does the we ... why ... wee ...nnnnnn ...er? How does the wiener feel inside your va .... va .... vag .... vague .... vay. I can't say that word, Susie. How's it go?" Charm was scarlet with effort.

"It says," I sat up a minute and took the crib notes away again, "it says vagina. See? V-A-G—that's vadge like badge. I-N-A is eye-na like Dinah Shore. Say it now. Vadge-eye-na."

Charm tried really hard. Vageenuh was as close as she could come. I lay back again. "Just say pussy. Forget that other thing. It's too tough for you."

"How does the wiener get into your pussy?" Charm got that right.

I knew my lines by heart. "The man gets on top of me and pushes it up inside the hole. It makes you sore and stings really a lot."

"Should I put the bottle in there now?" It was Charm's own voice again.

I sighed. "We're gonna leave out the bottle part." I took Charm's pudgy hand and said, "Press your finger right here ..." I directed her pointing finger to the spot, " ... an' rub up and down really slow."

Charm did as she was instructed. For what seemed like five minutes I lay flat out and moved against Charmaine's gentle touch. When I closed my eyes I saw Johnny Banks and his huge hardness. The flutterings in my tummy came again and again. Ocean waves, breakers the size of a house appeared before me. I saw the tall man in the park with his fly wide open exposing himself. I imagined my little brother Pete's peepee when it got all stiff. And I remembered watching two dogs fastened together on the neighbor's lawn the day before. Whatever flight of fancy befell my impassioned mind, I felt all wet down there.

"Do it harder. Push down more," I panted to Charm.

"It's growing!" Alarm had entered Charm's voice.

"It is not! Just press harder like I toldja," I said. The abrupt cessation of the rubbings had brought me out of my arousal. I craned my neck to get a look at Charmaine's face and said, "Why do you have to be so dumb all the time?"

Charmaine recoiled. "Okay for you, Susie. I'm not touchin' you anymore. If you don't believe me that it's growing bigger then ..." She grabbed my hand. "Feel it yerself." Charmaine placed my finger on my erected clitoris. "There! Ya see? I'm not kiddin'."

It was true. My formerly small, familiar little rosebud had grown to disquieting proportions. I leapt down from the table, forgot to fetch my underpants from under the couch cushion and raced, skirts in the wind, the five blocks home. Without so much as a "Hi, Mommy, I'm home," I flew up the stairs to the bathroom, bolted the door and sat down on the terrycloth toilet seat top to cry. Now, for sure, I was being punished. I knew I wasn't like good little girls. Good kids didn't get all swollen up down there. What would I tell my mother? What if they took me to the doctor? I was sure. It was God. This new deformation had to be God's way of showing me that my desserts would be just ... like Pinocchio's.

CHAPTER TWO

U pon advice from his Irish Catholic wife Elva, the rigorously Episcopalian George Hoskins Senior had paid tuition to Catholic high schools for his two eldest kids. He was determined to spare his teenage children contact with the greasy lower-class riffraff in South Buffalo's public high schools. By 1950, George Junior, the Rooster, and Sally, the Gypsy, were mostly off on their own teenage wavelengths.

Meanwhile, in her thirties, a few years after bearing me, Elva, the Lamb, had gotten pregnant several times. Only two of the pregnancies hatched. The first to materialize was Peter, the Dog, in 1946. Then four years later along came John, the Baby. Suddenly, minus the Gypsy and the Rooster, I was the head sibling. The chief kid in the household with two little brothers to care for and boss around.

Soon it would be time for me to go to high school, too. Like with the two older children, the Lion wanted to see to it I didn't have to rub shoulders with the working-class Irish and slovenly Italians and possibly be tainted by their intrinsic hooliganism. Anything would be better than condemning his baby daughter, Susie, to a life of Friday night fish fries and beer busts, married to some grease-ball wop or drunken mick without any dough. The Lion, however, did resist the idea of sending me to grapple with the Catholic nuns at Mount Mercy Academy. They had already done enough damage to the Gypsy's self-confidence by referring to her for four whole years as The Protestant. A suitable secular high school had not yet been chosen for me.

When the Lamb, age forty, was in the unwieldy advanced stage of her fifth infanticipation, occasions for me to shine above the others came along almost hourly. There was sweet-natured little Peter to be entertained and comforted. There were innumerable bike-riding trips to the store for my mother. I could present the neatly folded Buffalo Evening News for the Lion's pre-dinner reading. His favorite armchair pillows could be plumped, sidewalks could be shoveled, his place at the table specially set with three teaspoons and an extra fork for salad. Most pleasant of all the chores available was the care and feeding of Pesco, the family Airedale, whom all the children had begged the parents to buy, but nobody but me would feed, walk and clean up after. Not because I was a goody-goody. Because chores bought privileges.

Despite the Lion's preoccupation with where I would go to high school, I was far from ready to make the leap from elementary to secondary school. It only looked as though I was mature because I brought home high marks, had taken over Peter's toilet training and went dutifully to Sunday school to sing songs about how Jesus loved me because I was weak and he was strong. In some ways, I suppose, I seemed grown up. But privately, I was still wrapped in the bunny blankets of my childhood.

For my twelfth birthday I requested yet another dolly to add to my vast collection of thirty-three babies, ten dolls in national costume and one — my favorite — Aunt Jemima. My Aunt Florence, my father's eccentric twin sister, was my mother's rival for my father's time and affection. My mom only tolerated Florence. She thought of her as wacky. But Florence was a loving wacko who often protected and spoiled me. Auntie Florence had given me Jemima when I was eight. I loved that doll. She was unique. Jemima wore a full-length cotton skirt and had two heads. She was a foot-long rag doll with those two heads and, now that I think of it, four arms. The trick with Jemima was to flip her upside down. One head was a white girl's head. It had pinkish white skin and Caucasian facial features. The other head was that of a black mammy. Her skin was black and her eyes bugged out. The doll's skirt was reversible. On the white girl's side, it was pink dotted with small white flowers. On the mammy's side, it was plain go-work-in-the-fields dull blue. I cherished that doll.

So when I asked for another doll for my twelfth birthday, Elva, the Lamb, clucked and asked, "Don't you think you're a little bit old for dolls?" But I assured her, "It's the last time I'll ask for one, Mommy. I promise. The really last time."

I just knew that the big rectangular package Daddy had brought home the day before my birthday must contain the final coveted dolly.

There had been some mumblings between my parents after last night's meal about whether or not ten dollars was too much. Elva had said it sounded like too much. The Lion insisted, "It's a pip." And Elva agreed, "Well, if you think so ..."

All through my birthday dinner I eyed the big box in the center of the best tablecloth and urged it to be the most beautifully dressed Madame Alexander Baby Doll in the whole wide world. I would call her Elizabeth, after my Nanny Hoskins. If she had real hair, I would braid it. If she came without shoes I would knit some tiny booties. Even if my parents hadn't had enough money to get the big one with the white dotted Swiss dress that I had shown my mother in the Montgomery Ward catalogue, I made mental peace with the idea that the middle-sized baby doll with the pink organdy bonnet and beribboned christening dress would do just fine.

Right away after cake and ice cream, I jumped up and cleared the plates away to make room for the action. With a smug anticipatory grin on my face, I took the box to my place at the table, tore at the paper and opened it. There, in the bottom of the box, suspended from behind by her flaming, dyed red wig, was a twenty-four-inch Rita Hayworth doll. Rita's cerise satin evening gown was slit fetchingly up both sides, showing off thick, muscular legs to the groin. Her painted toenails glared at me like ten open wounds from high-heeled gold sandals. A sexy pouting mouth gleamed ruby-red against garish undertaker makeup. Ultra-long lashes, thick and heavy as rake prongs, were set off by gilded sequined eyelids. To make her even more attractive, the manufacturer had doused this curvaceous caricature with a generous dose of some synthetic floral perfume. A tiny glass bottle containing an extra ration of the potent scent was attached to Rita's wrist by means of a silver lamé elastic bracelet. A golden locket adorned the trollop doll's cleavage and read, "Hi, I'm Rita! Wanna Play with Me?"

In unison, the Hoskins family cheered the cleverness of the old Lion at having found such a pip of a doll as the final happy addition to my doll collection. "Isn't she lovely?" the Lamb inquired.

"What a piece!" exclaimed the seventeen-year-old Rooster.

"Hubba hubba on that red dress!" was the Gypsy's two cents. Four-year-old Peter watched my mouth quiver. My chair toppled noisily when I ran from the room. Little Peter blurted, "Susie wanted a baby."

Upstairs, I sat back to front, straddling the base of the Ideal Standard ceramic toilet and threw up my birthday dinner.

One wintry afternoon, shortly before the birth of my baby brother, John, my almost-sixteen-year-old sister Sally, the Gypsy, handed me a book entitled *Growing Up and Liking It.*

"Here," she said, tossing the thin green volume on my bed. "Mom told me to give you this. It's about where babies come from." I leafed through the pages and asked, "What am I supposed to do with it?"

"Read it, stupid!" said Sally.

"If it's about periods and stuff, I already know because Charmaine Cutler has hers and she told me," I said.

Sally replied, "It tells all about how your thing works down there. You know, labias and stuff. I read it when I was little. It's pretty good." Sally showered her pulse points in April Violets cologne, then headed off dancing somewhere chaste and permissible by the Lion's lights — either a church hop or a co-ed Girl and Boy Scout dance.

I opened the book to Chapter One, "Your Pubic Parts." Underneath the heading was an intricate line drawing of a lady's plumbing system. As my sister was leaving the room, I called after her, "What's so public about a vagina?"

The Gypsy hollered back, "Not public, stupid. Pubic!"

Straightaway the book was a disappointment. It wasn't about babies at all. But to give it a chance, for the next fifteen minutes or so I leafed through its pages, pouncing on every word or phrase which might quench my desire to find the solution to the still mysterious parts of life's biggest puzzle. The book's lack of plot or adventure was irritating, and the writing style stiff, repeatedly employing such terms as "mons veneris," "urethra," "fallopians," "vulvic regions" and "glans." Those words sounded like the names of countries in Asia, rivers flowing into the Danube or distant mountain ranges. I wasn't learning anything. *Growing Up and Liking It* was a tossed salad of incomprehensible terminology.

But there was a center foldout with tinted photos of a lady's pussy and, overleaf, a gentleman's wiener. I allowed as how these pictures were ample compensation for the bewildering rest of the book. After studying the images for a time, I collected the necessary accessories for prospecting: one small hand mirror, a flashlight, a medium-sized test tube from my chemistry set and a jar of the Gypsy's cold cream for a penetration test. Thus equipped, I made my way to the john, locked the door, spread the yellow bath mat on the floor and flattened the pages of my book. I was after an eyewitness comparison analysis of my own pubic regions with the author's photographed samples.

It was the first time I had ever looked at my privates. Though I had always enjoyed how they felt to the touch, visually examining intimate sections of my own body had always been off limits. Till now, the only pussy I had ever actually seen was Charmaine Cutler's. But that was boring because I had diddled Charmaine's bald pussy long before it grew pubic hairs or dreamed of having its period. On this memorable day, initially what my mother's round magnifying mirror told me about my pubic area was that mine was about ten times larger than the book lady's. Gingerly, I turned the magnifying mirror over to the non-magnifying side. *There now,* I thought *Let me see ...*

I opened the labias with my fingers. Majoras first. Minoras second. That part seemed okay. "Vulva" was a new one. It sounded a lot like my mother's name, Elva, and seemed to mean everything and nothing at the same time. "Hymen" was next. I could not for the life of me locate mine. Even assisted by the flashlight's glow, it was too dark inside there to find a membrane. I guessed my vagina was under there somewhere too. Still, the opening looked way too tiny to be doing business with the penis pictured on the overleaf.

Glancing at the test tube, I flipped the page to compare it to the size of that penis again. *How in the world?* The test tube was slimmer than the penis, for sure. I dabbed some cold cream on the very edge of what I thought might be the opening. I propped the mirror against the sink's porcelain bottom and stretched the majora lips open with two hands, positioning the flashlight between two fingers — just so. But no matter what, I could see for myself that actual penetration by a sausagey great penis was an impossibility. Nothing thicker than a darning needle could ever go up in there without ripping me apart.

I flipped back to the woman's pussy page again. There, I noted, was an arrow pointing to a muddy-looking area right above the supposed hole. That section was labeled "clitoris" in teensy lettering. Feeling around some more, I came upon my own hard spot. Was that my clitoris? If so, I was actually facing it for the first time. I was disturbed to find that my clitoris in no way resembled the flat one in the picture. Squinting at the image in the mirror, I could see there was something seriously askew. Mine was a double-nippled button, much bigger than even the grownup person's in the book. When I laid a finger directly on the spot, twinges of electricity shot through my arms and legs. And my stupid clitoris thing grew bigger.

Back when we had played YoYo, Charmaine Cutler had seen it swelling. I hadn't believed her. But now I could definitely see what was up. Life *was* exactly like the Pinocchio story. All that diddling and playing doctor with myself and Charm and Dickie and the boys in the bushes had been wrong and bad. You touched yourself down there and every time — exactly like Pinocchio's nose — your clitoris grew.

Then and there I determined I would stop playing with myself. Reading the whole book and taking a visual voyage into my personal underbrush had left me as mystified as ever about what "going all the way" with a boy might bode. Moreover, now I was scared. And ashamed. I wondered about Johnny Banks. He must have been touching himself since he was a little boy to have developed such a bludgeon. How big must his wiener be by this time? Then, I had a comforting thought. What if being good enough long enough could shrink whatever damage had been done? My heart warmed at that idea. But deep in my serious Sunday school self, I knew the jig was up. No use praying to Him and then waiting around for God to revoke the Pinocchio edict. He had never listened to my prayers anyway.

A knock came on the bathroom door. "Susie?" said a deep voice. "I need to get in there."

"Coming!" I hollered. I stashed my contraband under my sweater, grabbed the book, pulled up my panties, barreled out the bathroom door past my dad and scurried back to my bedroom.

All alone on my bed, I took stock. It was awful. I was only thirteen and I already had a clumsy overgrown clitoris. I would never be able to have a boyfriend. What if we went *all the way*? What if one day a boy touched me down there and discovered that my clitoris had grown to the size of an elephant's trunk? I felt tears welling up. I didn't want to go to Hell.

But the more I thought about abandoning my solitary diddlings, the more I wanted to continue. If I was already doomed to end up in Hell anyway, I might as well go on touching myself until the Devil came for me. I lay the sex book aside, pitched backwards on my twin bed, knees apart. I pushed down my panties and let my stubby, nail-bitten fingers wander inward from the labia, to stray momentarily in the valley of the vulva and then to creep northward toward my clitoris. The first touch of my index finger on the soft pink rosebud made me start. The double pleasure of my own skin on the slippery membrane sent a sizzling electric shock shuddering through my body.

Rising up on one elbow, I groped around the bedspread until I found the hand mirror. Then, resuming my diddling, I watched, intrigued, as my little hooded button crept slowly, like a drugged earthworm, out of its lair and winked a rose-white eye into the mirror. Contrasted against the purple-fleshy background, my clitoris looked as though it were preparing to deliver a speech or sing a little ditty into the looking glass. As it emerged, the opalescent rose grew ever more sensitive. Its skin stretched taut, as the fingerings grew urgent. The finger on the clitoris halted briefly while a giant wave of sensation crashed over my bed.

In its wake were delicate ripples. A calm sunny day at Crystal Beach. But I dared not dally. It felt distinctly as though there was more work to be done. My clit was still too big. And it had two sides. The first side emitted shock waves, the second, when I stroked it, gave a kind of localized burning sensation. Though the pinkish skin fairly ached from the heat, I turned to the lee side of my flower. Gently now because of the almost painful intensity, I prodded the edge with the flat ball of my finger, administering tense licks like the tiny beating of hummingbird's wings. More waves washed over me, and then ebbed, leaving a thirty-second space as in *station identification* on the radio. I grabbed the mirror and peeked at my face. It, too, was scarlet. And sweating big drops. A final glimpse before dying? I wondered if what they said was true. Could God really *see* everything? If He could, I was a dead doornail. But — if God didn't have eyes in the back of His head, I figured there might be room — some leeway — for a bit more exploration before he sent me to the Devil.

I returned to my game. My legs began to tremble. Another shift of the index to the right side of my burgeoning blossom engendered more delicious burning. Daggers of light streaked to my brain. Everybody was up there in my head, cheering and throwing bouquets of red roses, a bloom at a time, onto my writhing form. There was the Lion and Johnny Banks and the boys in school and Rita Hayworth and Charmaine Cutler's father and even Jesus himself. The intensity of the experience was such that it occurred to me I might actually be kicking some kind of bucket. Yet, as the adventure progressed, the swelling urgency felt less and less like dying. Instead, I felt throbbingly alive.

24

Should I pull through, I thought briefly, *this new discovery could be a significant step toward giving up baby dolls and Easter baskets.* The tender clitoris itself would no longer tolerate being massaged directly. But on I pressed, applying full hand pressure to the outer lips of my pussy. Back and forth, left to right, then up and down, faster and more wildly I rubbed the whole shebang. Knees up, eyes squinted tightly against the impending crash, I gave a final blast of speedy pressure on my swollen flesh and blew the brains out of my shame-addled head.

CHAPTER THREE

A s my teen years approached, I more and more perceived family life as a minefield. My elder siblings, George the
Rooster and Sally the Gypsy, had both hit paternal trip wires that
I was determined to avoid. The scenes, sparked off by the Gypsy wearing too much makeup, rolling in after curfew and riding in cars with
boys, were more and more thunderous. Her first year in college, Sally
had blithely flounced home to announce at dinner that she had been
cast as a call girl in an amateur theatrical to be produced by the
prestigious Blue Maskers troupe at University of Buffalo.

The Lion roared so loud the dishes rattled, wobbled and threatened
to topple off the table. "I knew it. I knew it. Didn't I tell you, Elva?
Girls don't belong in college. Those eggheads up there at UB will fill
her head with Communist crap. Next thing we know she'll be
dragging home niggers and wops and ..." He gave the tabletop another good bop with his fist and added, " ... and who knows what other
riffraff?" The Lion was growing a mane of sweat. "Sally, I won't
hear of you being in this play. I refuse to have my name on that
program."

"But Dad ... " said Sally, "It won't be *your* name. You're not Sally
Hoskins who plays Babe. *I* am." The Gypsy was scarlet. Her emerald
Irish eyes shone greener. "*I* am playing this part. Not *you!*" Tears
began sneaking down the Gypsy's freckled cheeks.

The Lion didn't slap Sally for talking back. He reset his rear end
into the head-of-the-table armchair and snorted. Gypsy heaved muffled, decorous sobs. Elva spoke up. "George ... " she tried, "Sally has
her heart set on being in this play. She gets to sing in it. Some very
pretty songs too. She has such a lovely voice. We can't very well
forbid her to do this."

Upshot was, Elva had to have a hysterectomy and big George gave
in to Sally doing the play. Still, he staunchly refused to allow the
Gypsy to put *his* Hoskins name on the theater program. So instead of
calling herself Sally Hoskins, Sally had the words "Sally Anne"
printed next to her character's name on the program. She thought
Sally Anne was a classier stage name than Sally Hoskins anyway.

As for the Rooster, thanks to his masterful skill at insubordination, he had been jettisoned and re-jettisoned from one Buffalo high school after the other. By the time he was sixteen, he had abandoned all attempts at studies and moved out to live on his own. Money? Young George made it. Wherever the Rooster went, he pecked away at some deal or other and hauled in the dough. When he was seventeen, he drove up to our house in a red convertible. He was wearing low-waisted black gabardine draped trousers with a chain where a belt would go and pointy black lace-up shoes. The Lion came outside, grabbed a glance at his son and proceeded to disdain both make and model. "Piece o' crap cars, these Fords. Tinny," he said, slapping the pristine ruby-red fender with his open hand. "Nobody drives a red car," he added. "Red cars are for hoodlums." As for the Lamb, she was relieved that her eldest son was still alive. I was mightily impressed by my big brother's bright red success.

The secret, I felt, to avoiding paternal eruptions was to resist dating boys and never to answer back. Hence, until age fourteen, I stayed sedately at home helping my mom by applying white polish to my baby brother's high-top shoes and bleaching the gray from the laces. I also scrubbed my sneakers and washed my woolen sweaters by hand in cold water. I occasionally practiced the piano. And I performed my undercover finger exercises clandestinely in my bed alone. Nowadays my meandering digits not only provided a physical charge, they also triggered images that held no resemblance to my real life. My girlish mind created characters and fancies that accompanied me on my private voyages into the unknown. The conjured creeps who traveled with me in my head were definitely not the sorts one would bring home to Dad. For a start, they were older — a lot older than me. Seedy slickers. Riffraff types who wore shiny clothes and drove glossy big cars. These were divided into two categories: henchmen and Boss. The henchmen were disreputable fellows who whisked me off the bus as I rode home from tap dancing lessons at the YWCA in the winter darkness. Sometimes my kidnappers were in cahoots with the bus driver. Once they abducted me on the walk home from my grandmother's house and threw me into a car. The henchmen were of course all dark-skinned foreigners and greasers with whom I was not allowed real-life contact. While seated on the upstairs john,

I would often sneak into the Rooster's behind-the-radiator stash of lurid Crime Does Not Pay comic books, wherein pretty women in off-the-shoulder blouses and tiny skirts were rendered helpless and treated brutally. Likewise, in my titillated pubescent mind, my own kidnappers executed brutal preliminaries such as striking me senseless with a lead pipe, blindfolding me and strapping me down on an operating table. Long story short, my conjured henchmen were scary guys. But I wasn't afraid of them. I fancied it didn't matter if I died at their hands. I was not my parents' child anyway. I was an adopted orphan.

"You want me ta club 'er again?" Jumbo was the oiliest henchman.

"Nah. She's out like a light." Lefty tightened the ropes.

"She's coming to, Lefty," said Legs. Legs was the lookout.

"She ain't goin' nowheres," said Lefty. "You better not scream, sister. Jumbo's watchin' you close."

I never screamed or struggled during these events. I knew full well that if I didn't let it all happen according to plan, there wouldn't be a happy ending. I did make little mental squeaking sounds when Jumbo came over and thrust his hand between my legs. But in the spirit of never talking to strangers, I remained mute.

"Relaaax, sister. Keep your shirt on." He felt around inside me, turned to his pals and wondered, "You think she's big enough to take on the Boss?"

Lefty answered, "He ain't worried if she ain't. He'll take her any-ways. She's skinny 'n young. Dat's da way he likes 'em." Lefty lit his frazzled cigar for the tenth time.

In delightful submission, I, of course, encouraged these fantasies, all the while twiddling away at my clitoris. To prolong the pleasure, I was always careful to remain on the brink of ultimacy. This trick was accomplished by prolonging the story's suspense. I was suitably wary of the henchmen. But not embarrassed. I did not mind one bit that they lurked about the cold, white room, watching me while awaiting the arrival of the Big Boss. Soon, the Boss came in, took off his overcoat and galoshes, hung up his fedora and beckoned the boys to a huddle in the corner. "The loot's at Simba's place. His wife's pretty so don't kill her, just rough her up a little," he might whisper to his henchmen, just loud enough for me to overhear.

At this, the Boss's boys picked up their respective bludgeons and

28

scampered off to Simba's place to reclaim their booty. The Boss never spied me immediately. I had put that little delay in on purpose to keep my clit lit. After a brief putter or two, the boss would look over at me and say, "Wait a sec, baby. I gotta piss." He'd pee in the sink, and zipping up on the way to the table he'd say, "Well now, ain't you a pretty little piece of ass." Before he had left home to become a teenage gangster, this "piece of ass" expression had been the Rooster's favorite dirty thing to say.

"I'm only twelve." I made myself sound terrorized. Gently stroking my body all over, Big Joe sat at my side and talked as I diddled. "With me, you ain't got nuttin' to worry about. You're the most beautiful kid I ever seen. Where'd they pick you up?"

"In the playground at school. I stayed out till after the streetlights went on. If I don't get home, my father's going to murder me." I had to prevent my index finger from creeping back into the wetness. If not, I would surely spoil my story.

"I'll take you home myself," said Joe. "Them guys of mine, they don't got no couth. You can tell 'em a hundred times, they never understood nuttin'. I couldn't fuck a little kid like you. I just like to look. Get it?"

I got it. I slowly let my hand find its way below again. Flicking my clit ever so skillfully now, I dared not press — or else. "So you aren't going to hit me or anything?" I said then. "Boy! Was I ever scared. Those men of yours are awful mean."

"Sweetheart, what I'd like to do is buy you a big, giant castle in *Parisfrance*. Like a princess. Couple of Doberman guard dogs, a few servants and closets of beautiful dresses with lacy slips hanging out. Dolls like you I don't git in here every day. You're a classy broad." Joe, the Boss, never even so much as got out a photo of his prick.

For me, this Boss mobster man was but a poor misunderstood gentleman in pig's clothing. I didn't mind a bit if he twiddled my pussy fuzz and put his tongue on my clitoris. Joe was the nicest gangster I had ever imagined. In the center of my cerebellum, bells and buzzers kept going off. I twirled my minoras around my clitoris. When I scrabbled this handful back and forth it felt a little like a huge tongue might. Before Big Joe could get in another word, I popped my rosy redness and winged my way to dreamland.

I got my period one evening while making fudge on our speckled green gas stove top. I was in eighth grade. Now for a week every month, I had to wear an elastic jigger attached to a gauze pad around my waist and under my pubics to catch my monthly wastes. The elastic itched and burned if I pulled it too tight, and if not — I risked having the whole bloody mess fall off in front of a boy! This humiliating monthly torture was termed "your little friend" by Hoskins ladyfolk.

"Does she have her little friend yet?" Aunt Florence snooped.

"How many days does Susie's little friend last?" Grandma Hoskins stuck her nose everywhere to ask.

Even Mildred Blank, the next-door neighbor, wanted to know, "Does Susie's little friend give her the cramps? My Shirley, poor thing, used to get the worst pains. Such a caution, that little friend business." In those days, the very mention of the word "friend" became intolerable to me. When I had cramps, my mother gave me brandy to drink and instructed me not to forget to soak my bloodied Lollipop panties in cold water right away so as not to set the stains. Today, fudge is still my *madeleine,* recalling to me that momentous episode in my little life when the first blob of warm sticky wetness arrived unannounced in my drawers.

Pesco, the Hoskins family dog, because of his size, his gamey odor and his incurable penchant for rolling in muck, had been exiled to the basement. The Lion had bought Pesco — and Pesco's pedigree — before Peter, the Dog was born. The purchase of a pedigreed dog was necessary to satisfy the Lion's secret image of himself as a country gentleman, stalking the vast moors of Cazenovia Park, outfitted to the teeth in tweeds.

Mr. Hoskins' Lord-of-the-Manor morning rambles with his pureblooded Airedale had lasted but a week. Pesco was all muscle and sinew. He yanked the leather leash taut, the Lion stumbled along after. He hurled children into mud puddles and growled and lurched at passersby. Pesco, moreover, frequently ran away. We Hoskins kids all wept. The Lamb wrung her hands in despair. The Lion roared. "Goddamn dog! Whose idea was this anyway?" The Lion demanded an answer from what remained of his assembled family. But none came forth. Bad luck also had it that when he did run away, Pesco always found his way home by midnight when he would sit outside the back door, wagging and howling to be let back in. Before the Lion could get out of bed and call the dog pound to come and take away the fugitive pooch that he would claim never to have laid eyes on, one Hoskins child or the other would take pity on Pesco and let the pathetic creature in the back door — only too delighted to hug the smelly cur and welcome him home.

Eventually the Lion caved in on the dog. "We are keeping Pesco," he announced. By accepting to retain the dog in residence, the Lion took it upon himself to teach Pesco not to escape. The solution? Beat him with a leather belt. Need we be reminded that it was not a total coincidence that Pesco bore the same name as the chain of new Buffalo supermarkets whose cutthroat price wars had recently cost the Lion most of his butcher shops' trade. The Lion beat Pesco without mercy.

While I loved Pesco, I also feared the Lion. I never mentioned that I had heard the frightened dog's yelps or that I had once even sneaked down and peered through the open backs of the cellar stairs to watch a monumental beating. The dog's eyes beamed neon yellow-green with terror. I had shuddered and silently wept. Now that the Rooster had quit high school and moved far uptown to become a rich hoodlum magazine salesman and the Gypsy was dating an older Italian up at the university, the Lion was carrying more than his usual share of stress.

I decided it was my mission to comfort Pesco. Following the thrashings, when the dust had settled, I would skip down to the basement, load some dirty clothes into the Bendix washer and turn the dial to its noisiest cycle. Then I would hunt around under the steps, in the coal bin or behind the fruit cellar for Pesco's cowering, shivering shape. Kneeling at his side, I would stroke my doggie gently and tell him what I thought of the Lion's cruelty. "He's a bully. He's twice as big as you. Next time, just growl at him really fierce. Don't stand there and take it. Jump him. Sic him. Bite him in the fanny."

With this, Pesco always came around to nuzzle me right where I liked to be nuzzled best. Pesco's IQ might not have been above average, but he definitely had a way with women. I found his gamey scent irresistible, his paws on my thighs perfectly adorable, and his tongue on my lickety clit devastatingly efficacious. I couldn't help it. I found fuzzy Pesco more attractive than any curly-haired boy I had ever met. Besides, he expected nothing in return for my affections.

"Maybe it's his frizzy fur," I thought as I made my way back upstairs. "Or could it be that softness under his belly?" Little matter what my attraction was about, the family dog kept me coming back for more. I knew he wouldn't rat on me.

As the affair between Pesco and myself progressed, our affections deepened. As in any good sexual relationship, intimacy and duration will improve the act of love. Over time, Pesco grew to know what I liked, how to seduce me with insistent nudges of the skirt, how long I liked his tongue to stay in one place before he paused for a breather. In a few months' time, Pesco had even learned to pull back the crotch of my panties with his teeth so he could access my privates. I wondered whether Pesco could one day become a famous circus dog. He might even go on the Ed Sullivan Show with me.

Once, on the way home from school, a big dog from down the street had jumped right on top of me with both front paws. All the kids laughed. They said he was trying to fuck me. I told them that was a disgusting idea.

I was yanking up my panties when I heard the basement door open. "Susie! You still down there?" cried the Lamb.

"Yes, Mommy," I answered.

"Bring up ten potatoes for supper, please." The basement door shut. I petted Pesco gently for a moment, then scrambled to my feet saying loudly enough for my mother to hear, "Now be a good doggie and don't run away anymore." I felt sorry leaving Pesco all alone in the chilly dark basement. But potato duty had summoned me back upstairs.

In the middle of my thirteenth year, Pesco caught a chill and suc-cumbed to the beckonings of the canine Jesus. I wept for over a week.

To my dad, the dog's departure meant one less mouth to supply with meat. As he'd been forced to sell his last and only butcher shop to the Mafia-controlled firm which ran the PESCO supermarkets, the Lion was job hunting. In the spirit of this chase he promised that, "as soon as Daddy gets back on his feet," he would buy me a Golden Retriever. The promise of a Golden Retriever was no consolation. I was despondent and quite certain, at thirteen going on fourteen, that the first great passion of my life was and would always be my beloved Pesco.

CHAPTER FOUR

T he Buffalo Seminary was a dream school. Two hundred over-privileged young women filled its hallowed halls for four of the most critical years of their lives. The school had been founded in 1851 as The Buffalo Female Academy. Gertrude Angell, a stern spinster dowager, had ruled the Seminary's roost from 1909 till 1952 when she retired, and an anonymous scholarship grant forced me to become A Seminary Girl.

I had taken the scholarship exam under duress. Winning the damn thing felt like punishment. My parents were proud. The Lion fancied I would be attending a finishing school where strict faculty members would teach me the rules of how to eat correctly, stop chewing my nails till I drew blood and cease picking my nose. I despised the very idea. I wept and pestered, pouted and threatened to run away from home. As a last ditch excuse I claimed that the two-hour bus ride each way every day would put me in jeopardy of kidnapping — or worse. But the parents demurred and enlisted me in Seminary's basic training.

I had secretly counted on attending public high school with my cronies from south of the Republic Steel plant. At South Park High, I would have learned how to type and take shorthand so as to grow up and become an executive secretary. But nothing doing. The Lion and the Lamb were in cahoots. They simply insisted I go to The Buffalo Seminary. No doubt about it. From the Lion's point of view, I needed finishing. From Seminary's perspective I was a gifted kid from the other side of the tracks who had aced their grueling entrance exam and earned herself a full tuition scholarship.

By 1950, at Seminary, dissenting members of the board of trustees had begun shouting Gertrude Angell down on issues such as enrollment quotas for Jews and the institution of scholarship funds for bright girls whose families had neither means nor lineage to recommend them for a Seminary experience. By 1952, the scholar-ship for deserving girls from the other side of the tracks allowed me to become a scholarship freshman. As Miss Angell was retiring, I slid in under the new rules. In September of 1952 Miss Angell was replaced by a fortyish woman with a dark, greasy bob. Her name was Miss Smith. She had gone to Wellesley. She wore navy blue blazers and gray skirts. And she smoked — incessantly.

During her reign, Miss Angell had held to be self-evident the following truths: all girls were not created ladies, most people were not Jewish, black people were not people, *nice* girls were debutantes, spoke from behind clenched teeth and joined the Junior League. Miss Smith was younger. She held fewer of Miss Angell's fusty views. Jewish girls could then apply to Seminary and the scholarship fund was expanded to include one or two clever poor kids, of which I was one.

At that time, it seemed that all the proper people had given their daughters names like Crinny, Tibby, Libby, Mimsy, Candy, Linsy, Bitsy, Betsy or Pert. Any deviation from this pattern — such as Patsy or Cecilia, Phyllis or Louise — was considered either *nouveau riche* or not *riche* at all.

The year I arrived at Seminary, on the first day of school, my freshman classmates and I were obliged one by one to rise and face our 199 schoolmates in chapel. Most of the shiny, well-born faces were framed by sleek, boyish blunt cuts. Bolstered by a life of entitlement and private schools, they crowed fearlessly through firmly clamped orthodontured chompers, "Hi! I'm Bitsy Letchworth — or Candy Goodyear or Mindy Kellogg — I'm glad to be at Sem." Most of them wore plaid kilt skirts from Scotland, Shetland sweaters from Best & Company, New York and circle pins.

They all had those elegant names. They lived on the upper west side of Buffalo. Their fathers were investment bankers, doctors, judges and lawyers. I was just Susie Hoskins. I was from South Buffalo and my father was a butcher.

That morning in chapel as my turn to speak approached, my blood stopped. There was but one other freshman scholarship student. She wore rimless glasses and a bright green blouse. When that girl stood to address the company of all those rich kids, I stared at her. *Who was she? Where did she live? What did her father do?*

"Good morning," voice cracking, feet shuffling. "I .... my name is .... um, uh, it's .... it's ... " The bespectacled girl opened her mouth to speak. But nothing much came out. A gray-haired teacher shushed the other girls' giggles. A rustling silence ensued. Then the new girl from the cheaper east side of town finally took a deep breath. Before she sat back down she managed to croak out, "I'm, I'm ... Shirley ... Poniatowski." Shirley was smart. And she was chubby.

I was dead scared. At hearing Shirley's unusual name, two hundred priceless old-family titters gilded the air. As I waited my turn, sweating,

I could not find a way to make "Susie" sound like anything but what it was: a dumb name for a kid from South Buffalo, a name for people who lived where steel plants belched and bowling alleys flourished amid the smog and soot, a name for people who didn't even know the word crumpet. I had been rehearsing in my head, "Hi there. I'm Susan Hoskins." It sounded moronic. So I tried, "My name is Susie Hoskins." That was worse. The girl next to me stood tall and straight. She had that private school lockjaw. Her name was Pussy Lockwood. And Pussy Lockwood was also "glad to be at Sem." She sat back down.

Inspired by what I assumed to be Pussy's daring nickname, I rose. Copying the others, I bit down hard on my own pink plastic orthodontic retainer and began, "Hello. My name is Clitsy Hoskins. I'm proud to be at Seminary." Nobody laughed. I swept up my circle skirt from behind like a proper lady and took my seat.

Without a hitch, the next well-heeled girl got to her feet, saying, "Hi! I'm Bambi Rumsey. I'm glad to be at Sem."

One evening, the telephone was ringing off its cradle in the front hall at the Hoskins House. On the tenth jingle, the Lion left the table in exasperated haste and lifted the receiver. Dinnertime calls were forbidden.

This call had been for "Clitsy." Returning to his place at the dining room table, the Lion harrumphed. "It was for somebody named Clitsy. A girl. Said her name is Melissa Rundell. For a wrong number, she sure has staying power letting it ring ten times." Taking fork in hand, the Lion murmured, "Rundell. Sounds Jewish to me."

I set my glass down and said, "Maybe you should have asked her."

The Lion snarled, "Don't get smart with me, young lady!" The Lamb interjected in her sweetest voice, "George, Melissa Rundell's father is a famous gynecologist. He's head of obstetrics at Buffalo General Hospital."

Spearing a rolling stack of elusive pork sausages, George Hoskins Senior muttered audibly, "Then he's Jewish all right. Makes a bundle."

Turned out those girls' names like Libby and Crinny and Bitsy were nicknames. They were short for longer, more dignified given names. Libby for Elizabeth. Crinny for Christa ... and Bitsy? Why Bitsy? Well, Bitsy was the diminutive for Butler. Her full name was Butler Edward Letchworth. I was surprised. Why would they call a girl Butler Edward? Obvious. Bitsy's great grandfather, Edward Butler, had founded the prestigious Buffalo Evening News. Therefore, Bitsy was named Butler Edward. Not something soft and fluffy like Eloise Butler or Heather Butler. Just plain Butler Edward. Bitsy's mother had married a Letchworth after whom they named a famous New York State park. So Bitsy got to be a pretty girl with a man's name. At home, nobody knew me as Clitsy. At Sem, everybody did. But nobody much knew what Clitsy was short for and I never offered an explanation.

Melissa Rundell, or 'Missy' for Seminary purposes, was indeed Jewish. In freshman year, she was to become my best friend. Missy was spoiled, acneyed, and shy. She wore thick glasses. On the other hand, Missy had a photographic memory, a gorgeous singing voice and an entire wardrobe of expensive cashmeres and circle pins in every metal that had ever been mined or invented. At home, she had her own private phone line. Dr. and Mrs. Rundell's phone number was Delaware 4000 and Missy's was Delaware 4001. Melissa played Bach on her home harpsichord and was driven to school by a white chauffeur until she was of age to drive her own sweet-sixteen, sky-blue Buick convertible with red leather seats and an oogah horn.

Seminary had allowed Dr. Morris Rundell to buy his way onto the board of trustees with a huge endowment for the school library fund and, in turn, Seminary had agreed to accept his Jewish daughter's application. This token acceptance did not, however, mean that Missy Rundell would be assured of a pleasant four years at Seminary.

Seminary was long on tradition and ethnic restrictions. Many of these were unwritten, dogmatic and pompous. The old guard had always felt a civic responsibility to see to the education of 200 young, white, Anglo Saxon Protestant girls within its walls. Until the Miss Smith-inspired revolution of 1952, no Jews or ethnics had been allowed to apply. When finally, a few outsiders were admitted, none would become candidate for field-hockey team captain or recruited for either of the school's two sororities.

Everybody at school agreed that Seminary's three or four Jewish girls were special. I knew this because Bambi Kellogg whispered to me one day in Latin class, "Missy Rundell is absent today. She isn't sick. It's one of *their* holidays."

The first time I met Missy Rundell, she was on the john. She and I had come down the oaken corridor from study hall as separately as two different cross-stitches on a gingham sampler. Missy raced ahead of me, let the huge wooden door of the lavatory swing shut in my face and quickly retired to the furthest enclosure, locking herself in tight.

Entering the next stall, I likewise slid the bolt to and sat. Our unison urinations created a concert of pitter-pats, but above these splashings I made out the telltale rustle of a Tampax paper envelope.

So Missy is a user, I mused, wishing that I, too, had a Jewish gynecologist father. Modess and Kotex period pads were inefficient and messy. I figured it was worth the risk of rebuff to find out how Missy managed to get one of those coveted cotton corks inside her. Even though the directions were supposed to instruct you, I had tried but was never able to get a cardboard tampon tube past the door to my vagina. I would have asked my mother, but she would have forbidden me to use them. Asking the Gypsy was out of the question. The Gypsy was a stickler for obedience and would snitch on me if she found out I had bought a box of Tampax with my allowance.

I dawdled in the cubicle, gathering my nerve. Then, gently, I knocked on the metal partition. "Excuse me, Missy. You don't know me. I'm Clitsy Hoskins. I'm … umh … was wondering … er … Do you have your period?"

I sucked in a breath and held it whilst Missy rolled out five or six feet of toilet tissue before answering. "Nope."

"Then how come you're putting in a Tampax?" I asked.

Missy flushed the toilet, exited her cubicle and politely added, "It's just some pesky discharge." She was washing her hands.

I pulled my undies up and joined Missy at the row of washbasins along the wall. This "discharge" business was a new one on me. It sounded military.

Over the noise of water splashing from the faucet, I dared, "What's a discharge, Missy. Please?"

Missy's face was tomato red. It was bad enough to be the daughter of a famous gynecologist who talked of nothing but fallopians and cervixes at the dinner table, now she was being asked to discuss medical matters at school as well. Next thing you know they'd be asking her to perform hysterectomies in the lunchroom. "I don' wanna talk about it," muttered Missy. She shook some of the excess water from her hands, rubbed off the rest on her skirt and started to leave the bathroom.

I did not let up. "Missy?" I repeated. "I'm really curious. I don't know. Can't you at least tell me what a *discharge* is?"

Missy rubbed her hands' remaining wetness on her pink cashmere sweater and blurted. "It's yellow and gunky and men can get it too, except it doesn't show up on them." She made for the door.

In hot pursuit, my own hands still dripping, I took Missy's arm halfway out the door. "I like you," I told Missy. "I want to be your friend."

Missy stopped dead. "Pardon me?" she said.

I pulled Missy back into the privacy of the lavatories. "I said I would like to be friends with you."

Missy was not a pretty girl, but behind her horn-rims she had lovely soft brown eyes. "You're the scholarship girl, aren't you?" asked Missy.

I nodded. "Yes. And I don't know many kids up here. My mother didn't go to Seminary. I'm from South Buffalo. I'm different from the other girls — a little bit like you, I guess."

"You're Jewish?"

Giggling, I poked Missy gently in the boob and twirled away from her to laugh. Then I said, "Of course not, silly. I'm Irish and English and Episcopalian. But I'm not really a Seminary girl. I mean, we live out in South Buffalo. My father doesn't own the steel plants either. We are just from there. My father was born out there." I stood picking at the clotted liquid soap on a washbasin top and mumbled, "I was just thinking that coming here from South Buffalo and being the poor kid — the scholarship girl — is sort of like being Jewish." I looked up at Missy and grinned.

Missy replied, smiling back. "I think I get it now," she said. She casually switched on the four hand-drying machines, one by one, along the wall. "You like me because I'm odd."

I pushed down the handle on a liquid soap dispenser and plopped a great gob of the yellow goo into the basin below. Winking at Missy, I continued to speak, "Well, I'm odd too. But maybe we're not as strange as we think. It might be *them* who are different." I pushed down the stopper and turned on the hot water in my basin full blast. Then I turned to Missy, pointing and sniggering as we watched the suds rise and overflow the sink's porcelain edge.

Missy chuckled, walked over to a second washbowl, pushed on its soap dispenser five or six times, smiling, "That's a crazy thing to say," she said. "It's very Jewish to think you're odd."

"Push down the sink stopper first!" I advised. Missy complied, gave a few more plunges on the soap dispenser's valve, opened the faucets wide and moved along to the next basin for a repeat performance.

In a fit of helpless glee, we stopped up drains, squished out soap and opened all eight water taps.

"Is Tampax Jewish?" I watched the bubbles rise in the final sink.

"It sounds a little bit Jewish, doesn't it?" Missy laughed.

"Come on!" I said. "We have to scram!" Pulling Missy away from her last sink, I gave each faucet a last twirl wide open and rushed out the door.

After the flood, meetings between Missy and me took place mostly at the scene of our crime — the school john. Neither of us was old enough to drive anywhere yet. Occasionally we shared Cokes and peanut doughnuts at a nearby drugstore after school. But usually we both had to hurry home so as not to be late for supper.

Next time I had my period, Missy was squeezing a zit onto the middle lavatory mirror and said, "Boy! I look like Alice in Pimple Land."

I, straddling the toilet in the open-doored stall behind Missy, wielded an unwrapped junior-size Tampax and begged her, "Missy, please! Can't we talk about your pimples later? You have to help me figure this thing out." Spread on the floor at my left foot were the complex graphic instructions on the use of Tampax for teens. Despite having probed at myself at least three hundred times, pamphlet in hand, leg raised on edge of toilet or chair, my fourteen-year-old self was no closer to introducing that arid cardboard cylinder into my teenage vagina than I'd been at age seven.

Missy turned toward me and instructed, "You're up too high, Clitsy. Put your finger in first. The hole has got to be there some-where. I asked my father. He says everybody's got one."

Pushing harder and once again meeting with only pain and irritation, I was dismayed. I was abnormal. I wanted to cry. "I know he says that. But Missy, your dad hasn't seen every single girl in the whole city of Buffalo. Maybe I'm ..."

"Oh, yes he has. Sooner or later my father gets to see them all. And let me tell you, if there's anything my father doesn't know about girls it's something they haven't invented." Missy was on sure ground. She said, "The bell's about to ring. Just go ahead and push it in. We have to get to Latin or Miss Darling will murdelize us!"

I sighed. "I can't. It won't go."

Missy scolded. "Oh Clitsy, will you please stop being such a sissy. You can't hurt yourself. It's just a hole — like your nose. It's what it was invented for in the first place. Just jab it up there and come on." Missy picked up her books.

I forced the paper tubing halfway into my parched pussy and begged Missy to wait. I stood up, flushed the instructions down the toilet, grabbed my own books and waddled along, in punishing agony, to our next class. For a full hour, I sat on one buttock, beseeching the lord not to allow the cardboard tubes to slip out on the floor when I stood back up.

Missy claimed she didn't really mind being blackballed by both Seminary's sororities. But her mother did. Mrs. Rundell longed to be able write a letter to her sister-in-law in Brooklyn, to boast of Melissa's acceptance into a WASP sisterhood. Against Missy's wishes, her mother phoned the headmistress. She insisted Missy be invited to join one or the other of the sororities and, if Miss Smith refused, Mrs. Rundell threatened to withdraw her husband's financial support from the Library fund.

This pushy, if well-intentioned, interference on her mother's part only served to ostracize Missy further. The word got around that Missy's mother was poking her big Jewish nose into the school's private business.

After that, nobody except me would speak to Missy. As fellow outcasts, we bonded, giggled and whispered all manner of slights and calumnies against the Seminary in-crowd. Missy knew of my avid interest in matters sexual. In a fit of gratitude for my loyalty, she stole a juicy professional sex book from her father's medical library and sneaked it into my possession.

That weekend, I spent two full days hidden in my room perusing in depth this inspirational book: *Sane Sex Life and Sane Sex Living.*

I felt privileged. According to the introduction, the book was sold only to doctors. It was not for public consumption.

This volume had been written by a Dr. H.W. Long. Dr. Long's revelations were so astounding and titillating that I neglected all of my homework and hardly spoke to my family members for forty-eight hours. From time to time, laying the book aside, I would plunge my hand into my pants, jiggle against it until the wetness flowed and then, without surrendering to time-consuming fantasies, I would return to the study of another gripping chapter of *Sane Sex.*

In his chapter on Sex Organs, Dr. Long listed the following:

"Male sex organs are penis and testicles. Female sex organs are vulva, vaginal passage, womb, and ovaries."

I was confused. Dr. Long's book was from 1869. Maybe they didn't know about clitorises back then. Or maybe my clitoris *was* the exception. I certainly knew that a clitoris was part of *my* sex organs. And I knew that it grew bigger when I stroked it and that it gave me those electrifying explosions that I had learned to love. Once again, though, I thought perhaps I was not normal. Maybe I had altered my original sex organs with too much diddling. According to Dr. Long, other females had vulvas and vaginal passages and wombs and ovaries — over and out. But it was plain to see in this "professionals only" book, that normal people's female sex organs did not include clitorises.

The book did, however, offer volumes of information. It started out with a loud message: "All Sane People Ought To Know About Sex Nature And Sex Functioning, Its Place In The Economy Of Life, Its Proper Training And Righteous Exercise."

That seemed a worthy approach. I delved further. I read Dr. Long's in-depth chapters on: Function of The Sex Organs, The Act of Coitus, First Union, The Art Of Love, Coitus Reservatus, Cleanliness and even Pregnancy. I skipped the Conclusion because it was late Sunday night and I had school the next day. Besides, I didn't need Dr. Long's Conclusions. After such an intensive study of *Sane Sex Life And Sane Sex Living*, I had drawn my own conclusions.

"Hi, Missy," I said from the privacy of my parents' upstairs telephone extension. "It's me."

"What's up?" asked Missy. "I can't stay on long. My father restricts my talk time."

"Did you say your mother preferred the Eta or Theta sorority?" I hurried.

Missy answered, "Why don't we just forget that whole sorority deal? My mother's all right now. She's dyeing her hair again. Instead of paying for the sorority, they're going to buy me a nose job and a horse."

Disappointed, I sighed, "Oh, crud! I had a perfect plan for getting you in, too. Are you sure your mother wouldn't change her mind?"

A strange beeping sound came on the line. Missy spoke quickly. "I have to go. That's my father's signal. He's cutting us off. See you in school." Click.

Next morning, I got the early bus uptown and arrived at Sem in plenty of time to stash *Sane Sex* in my locker. At lunch break, I met Missy in the lav and clued her into my strategic plan. I would collar every senior Goodyear, Kellogg, Pringle and Prendergast I could get my hands on and confide that Missy Rundell had a huge sexy book with every single position, dirty word and drawing that any girl could wish to know about — right in its pages! Black and white, color plates, photographs and details hitherto undreamed-of figured in this book. The trouble is, I shook my head sadly as I told Pipsy Higgenbottom the good news, "It's Missy's private property. And Missy absolutely refuses to show it to any girl who belongs to a sorority."

Missy was aghast. "My father will have a cow. He doesn't know I lent you his book."

"Your father doesn't have to know. The book is safe in my locker," I told her. "Don't worry, Missy. I have everything under control."

The word was out. By Wednesday, the presidents of both Eta and Theta had tracked me down. It wasn't fair, they argued; nobody had the right to withhold vital information from a senior class member. It was insubordinate. "Melissa could get a load of demerit slips out of this," they cautioned.

I knew that, in principle, because the seniors ran the school's judicial system and held weekly courts wherein they punished girls for wearing loafers that scratched the wax on the hardwood floors, gave them hours of dull compositions to write for chewing gum in chapel and made them pay steep fines for forgetting their regulation black stockings under their gym tunics — they might be able to blackmail the book from Melissa.

43

But I was prepared for this eventuality. My answer to Libby Kittinger, Sissy Standish and Mimsy Rockwell, who were among the most senior students of all, was just this: "If I heard that Missy got a demerit slip from a senior, I guess I would have to go straight to Miss Smith and tell her why you all knew about the stuff inside the book in the first place. Must mean you saw the book, right?" The seniors decided then and there that they would rather have a look at Missy's book of sexy secrets than see her punished.

By the following Monday, Missy Rundell had more new friends than Jesus on his birthday. Piles of handwritten engraved cards invited her to pledge teas and luncheons in her own honor.

Three weeks later, when Missy was on the brink of becoming the first Jewish girl in Seminary's history to wear a green blazer escutcheoned with the Eta crest and piped all around in yellow braid, Miss Smith called a special after-school chapel session to announce, "For the purpose of encouraging democracy among the student body, I have decided to abolish the outdated practice of rival sororities. From now on, you are all requested to abstain from discussion or activities pertaining to Eta or Theta. No more yellow or green blazers. No more rivalries on the sports field. As of today, sororities at Seminary are a thing of the past. It is hoped each of you will conform to this new rule with the singular grace and dignity worthy of a Seminary girl."

In a single speech in chapel, Miss Smith had outlawed sororities which, of course, precluded Missy Rundell being invited to join either Eta or Theta. The war was over. Nobody had won.

CHAPTER FIVE

A t sixteen going on seventeen, being a flat-out teenager struck me as complex and burdensome. To stick to the rules, I had to pretend I was still a kid. Obedient. Compliant. Respectful. But in my head I was none of those. I was defiant. Feisty. All grown up. The Lion was more and more irritable in my regard. He claimed he was worried about me. Was I ever going to be ready to marry a doctor? Would I ever learn to sit up like a lady and take my fingers out of my nose? Would I stop chewing my fingernails to the quick before my sister's wedding?

That same wedding, by the way, was not the Lion's favorite subject. In an antique Neapolitan lace wedding gown with a spangled floor-length veil, the Gypsy married Tony Potenza, a Dean Martin look-alike who was attending her university on the GI Bill. Tony was older. But that was not the worst of it. Tony was Italian. To my father's low church Episcopalian sensitivities, the Gypsy's gaudy wedding ceremony at St. Paul's Cathedral in downtown Buffalo epitomized ostentatious social climbing. But although he bellyached, the Lion paid for his number one daughter's wedding.

That same season, the Rooster wed Thelma Martinelli, a pretty nursing student, whose parents worked downstate at the Corning Glassworks factory. This time the Lion only had to pay for the flowers. Nevertheless, the fact that Thelma's immigrant Sicilian parents did not speak English further exacerbated the Lion's chronic heartburn.

Elva repeatedly reminded her husband, "The Potenzas are respected members of the Italian community here in Buffalo," and "The Martinellis are simple, hardworking people who came from nothing and are sending their daughter to school away from home. All by herself."

"Yeah. But if they'd kept her home down there in Corning, our George wouldn't have married her, would he?" retorted the Lion. "How can I explain a slew of dago grandchildren to my friends at the Masonic Lodge or the Buffalo Athletic Club? Goddammit, Elva! Our kids'll be eating spaghetti for Thanksgiving!"

Thanks to the two Lion-shattering marriages, my own social life was suddenly cluttered with new restrictions. I was allowed to go out on dates. I was even permitted to accept invitations for church dances and hayrides from boys. However, the Lion had declared that I could not date Polacks, wops, Czech, Russian, Hungarian, French or — well, it went undiscussed but obviously not with *niggers*. To emphasize these strictures, my dad sat me down one evening and delivered his famous *Ethnic Embargo Speech* of 1954. Our meeting took place in the Rooster's old bedroom. The one with the Scotch plaid wallpaper. The Lion had commandeered it as his office. I was nervous, leery of what further edicts The Lion might have in store. Dad's feet were propped on the desk. He leaned back in his springy office chair and said, "This great country is made up of all kinds of wonderful people. Rich and poor alike. Many of them came to our shores to escape poverty and found opportunity. We took them in, gave them housing and jobs and welcomed them into our fine schools and churches. Now they have more than they ever hoped or dreamed of having. Full bellies and a roof over their heads. They eat our American food, drink our beer, swim in our municipal swimming pools and are cared for by our fine doctors. Unfortunately, many of these good folks are not even a generation away from being dirt poor. They haven't developed the brains to learn our language or to adopt our ways. Many of them don't even know our national anthem or the Pledge of Allegiance all the way through. They are like children. Their homes are infested with roaches and their clothes … well, just look at their clothes." He paused for a breath, and I glommed onto the opportunity for a brief escape. I raised my hand.

"Dad?" I interrupted. "Can you wait a sec? I have to pee." I got up to leave the room.

"Don't say pee! Say you have to go to the *bathroom*," roared the Lion. "And don't tell me what you're going to do in that bathroom either. You might be going to the bathroom for … for ... I don't know …. for, say, a Band-Aid. It's none of my business why you're going to the bathroom. Can't you understand that? People don't need to know your bathroom intention. Skip the details. From now on, just excuse yourself to *go to the bathroom*."

What next? I thought, and trotted along to the john. I sat musing atop the open toilet, a-bristle with the temptation to put finger to clitoris in reckless postponement of the unadulterated boredom I knew awaited me on the other side of my father's desk. I even toyed with the idea of returning to the Lion's den wearing a Band-Aid over my mouth. I left that idea to rot and piddled into the toilet.

Before returning to my father's office, I caught a glimpse of my face in the bathroom mirror, paused and gave myself a pep talk. "Susie, you are a prisoner in the kingdom of the Band-Aid People. You must try to escape. But whatever road you take will be guarded by Band-Aid-wielding sirens whose voices will ring out alluring promises of safe harbor, easy street, chubby babies, true love, church picnics, a steady boyfriend for life, a house to clean and money to burn. To ensure that you don't stay entrapped, Susie Q, you must keep all your senses alert. Otherwise the Band-Aid People will sneak into your room while you sleep and paste one of their indelible HOUSEWIFE Band-aid stickers on you. And once that label has been planted, it will remain forever glued to your person."

Shuddering, I pulled myself together and went back for the next installment. When I opened the door of the office, the Lion looked up, "I thought you fell in," he chortled.

I sat crossed-ankled, prim, finishing school style, pulled my skirt down over my knees and batted my lashes. I said nothing.

Shoving his pencil behind one ear in true butcher style, the Lion sat up straight and thought aloud, "Now where was I? Oh, yes, *kikes*." He adjusted the slant of the pencil two or three times before going on. "What I want to say to you, young lady, is this ..." Hands clasped atop the desk, he made circles with his thumbs, cleared his throat and said, "Same goes for Jews ..." He passed his right hand over his bald spot and made another *ahem* noise. Then, shaking his index finger in the direction of my face he warned, "Girls who marry foreigners can't get into hotels in Miami. They can't join country clubs or eat in decent restaurants. They can never get elected president of the PTA. I'm not even sure that people with foreign names can fly on American Airlines." He lowered his finger, sat back and added, "There are a few exceptions. If a Jew's father is a doctor or a lawyer, you can probably go out with the guy. Otherwise no Jews. Is that clear?"

Lying through my orthodonture, I answered, "Okay, Dad. I promise." I hunted through my synapses for an explanation as to why I had inherited the wrong end of an ill wind.

As I lay abed at night, I pondered what slim possibilities for romance I might have if I never risked dating a jungle bunny, a greasy spic, a yellow-bellied Jap, a fat wop greengrocer or a dirty Jew. If every time a boy asked me out, I had to insist he recite the Pledge of Allegiance all the way through, sing The Star-Spangled Banner and commit "amber waves of grain and purple mountains' majesties" to memory, the boyfriend pickings would remain mighty slim.

I was never going to meet any Jewish doctors' sons at my weekly Saint Simon's Church's Young People's socials. I never came close to encountering any uptown boys — the kind whose sisters went to Seminary. I lived in a working class neighborhood in South Buffalo. In the real city of Buffalo, the merchants were mostly Jewish, the labor force was a good seventy-five percent Polish, the intellectuals were married with six kids and no money — and the mayor was Italian. Who in the name of the great Lake Erie did the Lion deem worthy to take me to a square dance if it wasn't somebody I might possibly meet in my own home town?

As always, the worst moments of anxiety over my future were soothed by fingering caresses of my genitalia. Clitsy Hoskins was, by now, a dedicated diddler. This self-absorbed intimacy, though still physically limited to the clitoral coastlines, was practically never entirely solitary. Since the death of Pesco, I had welcomed scads of new phantom characters into my head.

There had been Louie, the greaser garbage-man, who always smiled at me from the truck on my way to catch the early bus. Every morning Louie greeted me the same way calling out from the back of the truck: "Morning, Glory. See the reindeer?"

I always giggled and scurried by. I saw no harm in inviting Louie into my fantasies. I enjoyed our innocent six-month relationship. Nobody — even Louie — had to know.

After Louie, I had mentally entertained Danny Battaglia, the Niagara Frontier Transit bus driver, whose route I rode five days a week every week of the school year. Danny was unique in my fantasies. I not only used him for imaginary stud purposes, but he had also assumed the unusual role of procuring other imaginary foreign men from among his passengers who might enjoy my favors.

For me, tickling my clit and making up sexy stories was good, clean fun. But as I neared seventeen, I was beginning to feel a profound need to flout my father's new rules beyond a mere mental fling with an Italian bus driver. In his stead, after a few fallow nights of searching for just the right fantasy came Danny Battaglia's replacement, Dr. Angelo Salvo. Dr. Salvo was a famous Italian scientist from New York City whose grandmother had been a Negro slave. Salvo was short. But lovable. He was dark-skinned and exotic. He smelled of tropical spices. Moreover, my Dr. Salvo was extremely dangerous.

In his laboratory, the good Dr. Salvo was involved in a research project. His experiments demanded secret implantations of healthy Italian sperm into the twats of white girl volunteers like me. He performed these tests with bare hands and novel instruments in the persons of a staff of live-in stud slaves. These were Frankenstein-like lackeys who groveled when he called. There was no need to make an appointment with Dr. Salvo. I simply had to press the pleasure button between my slippery minora and Bingo! I was inside Doctor Salvo's laboratory like a shot.

Most nights now, I would fantasize myself strapped to Dr. Salvo's laboratory table, rigid with fear and hopelessly excited. "So, you are here once again, my dear," he would say, rubbing his hairy hands together. His rimless glasses had been taped together with Band-Aids.

By altering my own voice to a higher pitch, I thought it would be easy to imitate the voice of Dr. Salvo. "Who shall I call on?" I squawked. My rendition of Dr. Salvo's crackly evil voice wasn't very convincing.

Making it up as I went along, I might tell the doctor, "The tall one with the big ears will do nicely, thank you. I like his big dick." Since there were several zombie-like studs to choose from — and they were the kindest, most gentle zombies you could ever want to meet — I always opted for whichever type came into my head first.

"Shall I spread you with my potion?" buzzed the good doctor.

At this point I slathered my pink rosebud with Pond's vanishing cream from a thirty-nine-cent jar I had bought out of my own money. "I don't think it can do any harm," I agreed.

"Big Ears!" the mad doctor would command. "Come see the nice cunt I have for you today." The tall creature lurched from the wings of my mind's eye on cue. "Big Ear like pretty lady. Big Ear want fuck pretty lady. Big Ear hungry pretty lady." From his manner of speaking, I could tell that Big Ears had not invented gunpowder. But I sensed he was a decent sort. Tall and burly, wearing a well-tailored pea-green zombie cloak, he spoke quite haltingly. But that didn't bother me. I wasn't planning on discussing much with Big Ears anyway.

"There now, Big Ears," said the good doctor. "You just whip out your enormous dick and shove it up the nice lady's hole." Doctor Salvo had occasional unprofessional lapses and employed coarse language. His filthy slips of the tongue excited me.

I slowed my finger to a light stroke and held my protective lips open

49

so Big Ears could get his huge dingus in. "I'm ready, doctor," I gasped.

At this, my index finger sometimes cramped and faltered. But by the grace of God and a double-jointed ring finger, I got going again and was shortly at fever pitch. The hulking freaks I had invented for these moments pointed their sausages directly at my privates. But their fingers and cocks and my fingers diddling away in the same venue created a kind of sexual traffic jam down there. I sorted out the jam-up by bringing myself to climax. Big Ears never penetrated me. In my fantasies, nobody's wiener had gotten inside. Like Tampax. They were rejected at the playground gate.

In this way I managed to remain a pure and healthy red-blooded American virgin. There were boys aplenty in my life. Guys from church and nice white boys I had met on the hour-long bus rides going back and forth from home to Seminary every day. I had invited one or two of them to the house for some iced tea or to listen my Dad's Benny Goodman records. But the Lion never approved of them. "Those boys you bring over here are all after just one thing," he said.

By this time, that "just one thing" was precisely the just one thing I was most curious about. I may have been mentally sleeping around with packets of weirdoes since I was old enough to reach my private parts, but I had never actually been touched down there by a human boy.

I was more than eager. But there were so many rules. How could I ever get a boyfriend who would kiss me and touch my skin and say *I love you* like in the movies? I was about to give up, when a thickset, swarthy guy with curly black hair grab-assed me in the bus one morning. He was probably Italian and Catholic. He was definitely older, like maybe eighteen. His name was Sam. Everybody knew he went to Tech High School and had flunked two grades. I liked him. He was kind of ... foreign. As in *dangerous*. One day, Sammy asked me what I was doing on Sunday night. I told him I always went to my Young People's Fellowship at church on Sunday evenings.

He jumped at the chance and offered to meet me in the parking lot behind the church that Sunday night. I had a funny feeling that Sammy was savvy about girls. So I agreed to meet him. It was high time I had my first kiss.

At seven-thirty, I spotted Sammy's Chevy coupe from the parish hall window. Without stopping to don my coat against the icy-cold Buffalo winter, I ran outside and hopped into the passenger seat.

"Hi!" I smiled at Sammy.

"You got here, huh?" Sammy, without looking at me, placed his big hand on my skinny thigh.

I lifted the hand from my leg and took it in mine, saying, "Cold, huh?"

Sammy wrenched his fingers from my clutch and replaced them uppermost on my flank. "How long you got?" he asked.

I blinked and said, "They've just gone into the church for the service. It's only the Young People's Society so it doesn't take more than about twenty minutes." Sammy's hot hand felt to me like the steel plate of a Sunbeam steam iron set at asbestos for smoother pressing. The car radio was playing Joni James singing, "Hold me. Hold me. Never let me go until you've told me, told me, what I want to know." I hummed along.

Sammy still said nothing but proceeded to knead the flesh on my upper leg, as though testing for doneness. I then said, "You're pretty fast for a guy from around here." And once again I attempted to pry his insistent, hot hand off my body.

But Sammy had not come to meet me in this god-forsaken church parking lot so we could play gin rummy. He muttered something under his breath and followed it up with this: "Come over here and tell me about the guys from around here. How do they do it? Is it anything like this?" Before I could utter another syllable, Sammy's hand was inside my sweater, blouse and bra. The worn leather of Sammy's jacket was crackly against my cheek. His duck's-ass hairdo smelled of Wildroot Cream Oil. There was an unfiltered cigarette behind his right ear and a whopping puddle in my underpants. I grew even more excited when Sammy plastered my mouth against his and began chomping at my lips. *This must be the way experienced boys kiss.* I thought. But I was rapidly disabused of this notion when Sammy's large, rough, muscular tongue pried open my clenched teeth and he commenced sucking on my own sweet velvety tongue. Sammy had powerful cheek muscles. I thought about the epileptic girl's fit in the drugstore soda bar last Sunday. We had stuck a pencil in her mouth so she wouldn't choke on her tongue. Would I choke on his tongue? I didn't have time to stick a pencil down my throat right then, but I finally managed to extricate my mouth from Sammy's using a growling technique I had not yet really perfected. But I did have a hunch my muffled growls might make him think I was suffocating. Then I'd be dead and he'd be arrested. He loosened his grip with a wet popping noise. My lips were sore, but free. By the time I regained the use of my aching tongue, Sammy's hand was swimming through the puddle in my drawers. Had I been in a drive-in movie parking lot with acres of cars around, I might have given in to my urge to scream. But I knew that a screaming young God-fearing woman in a '38 Chevy coupe with a dusky young man would have been way out of order on church-owned property. So I sighed instead and heaved my buttocks a bit closer to Sammy's side of the car, saying, "You won't hurt me, will you?"

By this time, Sammy's index had found my clitoris. Two of his other fingers were inside my vagina and he was talking to me in a surly, calculated whisper. "Does that hurt?" He said as he plunged the ring and pinkie fingers deeper inside. Then, wriggling his index finger atop the fleshy rosebud with which I was so familiar, Sammy told me, "Just relax. This only takes a minute."

Not a bad minute, I thought as I humped against the outspread palm of this boy wonder I had so erroneously taken for a slob. I drew my tightness around his hand. He pushed harder and twiddled faster until, out of the blue, my soul became one with my mind and body in a long gush of gorgeousness unlike anything I had ever imagined or dreamed might exist.

I tilted my head back on the scratchy plush seat to recover. Then Sammy's voice came over loud and clear. "Button up now. It's my turn." Sammy short-ordered his sex: "One hand job on toast, hold the mayo. One hot dog straight up." And straight up he was — ready for the crunch.

I had never even seen a grownup boy's whatchacallit. And this was not about to be my chance. The car was full of dark. I could only grope recklessly in the direction of his unzipped fly and so unwittingly slapped the poor fellow's member with the back of my hand.

"Holy shit! Be careful, will ya?"

"Oh, gosh. I'm sorry. Are you hurt?"

I had brought Pesco off this way a few times. Gently. But this sudden contact with real human flesh had made me feel terrifically jazzed up and tense. I grabbed Sammy's prick as though I were about to make a telephone call with it and rapidly tried to recall what Dr. Long had advised in the Sane Sex chapter on hand jobs.

"Just take it easy. Slower and real easy." Sam kept spitting in his hand and trying to put the spit on his hard-on. But I was in the way.

Instead of adding slide to the mix, Sammy just kept dropping drool all over my wrist.

Surely you didn't just come right out and ask someone how to jerk you off. That would be repulsive. But the more I tugged and pulled and pushed, the more uneasy I became and the tighter I gripped until finally Sammy tore my clumsy, nail-bitten hand away and spat directly from his mouth into his cock's eyeball. Giving himself three whacks, he let out a yelp, sprayed my Villager Classic sweater with bleachy-smelling jism and reached over my lap to open the car door, saying, "Go back to church where you belong!"

I never saw Sammy again. But over the years as I grew more experienced, questing in vain for the giant orgasm in the sky, I often wondered where in the world that Sammy guy from the crosstown bus had found out about girls and their rosebuds. And I was dying to know with whom he was doing all those lovely things now.

CHAPTER SIX

Before graduating from Seminary, I had to pass the student-created Purity Test, land a decent slot in the senior poll, attend a deb party or two and pass my College Boards.

On the Purity Test, the girls who developed the questionnaire asked things like how many times you had been French-fingered, French kissed, performed a blow job, had more than ten hickeys on your body at any given time and what size Tampax you wore. Not one question said anything about being licked by a dog, invited to Paris by a gangster named Joe, plunged into by zombies under the tutelage of a fiendish Italian-Negro scientist or frictioned to paradise in a parking lot by a swarthy hood. I lied about the super Tampax, which put me ten points ahead of Bunny Goodyear and Bitsy Letchworth, who only scored twenty points out of a hundred because they thought the whole thing was disgusting.

Surprisingly, Melissa Rundell got the highest score. Missy, it turned out, purported to have performed twenty-one blow jobs, gotten thirteen hickeys on her neck and shoulders and had actually swallowed cum three times in her own automobile. Once, she wrote, she even wore two super Tampaxes at the same time! Missy's score proved it — maybe Jewish boys were really hot. If only the Lion hadn't been so averse to my dating Jewish boys, I might have gotten a higher score on the Purity Test. My score was pitiful by comparison to Missy's.

All of the seniors had to vote for each other in the senior poll. We chose from categories such as who would be most likely to succeed or who would be the first married or who would become a lawyer etc. Not everyone got chosen for something. So I was thrilled when I found out I had received enough votes from my classmates to be designated "Class Clown."

I galloped home waving my official Class Clown certificate and left it on top of the mail on the desk in the living room so my dad would see it when he got home from work. At supper, we were, as usual, all seated quietly around the dining room table. It was evident the Lion was in a feisty humor. The air in the room gave off high-tension-wire vibes. I spoke up first. "Daddy?" I started. "Did you see I got Class Clown?"

George Senior slowly consumed his pineapple and cream cheese with walnuts salad starter. We watched in silence.

"Dad?" I said again. "I got Class Clown." I was pleased. My schoolmates not only thought I was funny. They voted me the funniest. The actual Class Clown.

The Lion set down his fork, propped his wrists on the table's edge. His eyes squinched. There was steam rising from his bald spot. He looked down at the table and muttered, "I send my kid to a private girls' finishing school and after four years of finishing, what does she become? Valedictorian of the class? Nope. Not my Susie. My Susie spends four costly years of my life to become the CLASS CLOWN." He took a sip of his iced tea and resumed cutting his gray roast beef.

Was I soft in the head? Whatever had made me imagine that my father would approve of me being class clown?

When I was half past sixteen, I got a part time job. At home, we were eating fewer lamb chops and more hamburger. One by one, the Lion closed his butcher shops. Supermarkets had ruined his business. The family needed me to bring in my own spending money to keep up with the extras attendant upon my going to school at swanky Buffalo Seminary. The wardrobe items alone: Lady Hathaway shirts, Weejun loafers, Spalding saddle shoes and circle pins. Moreover, you couldn't get by with only one pair of those expensive thick Wigwam socks because you had to wash them by hand at night and they took two days to dry. A real camel hair polo coat with mother-of-pearl buttons could set one back fifty dollars, and party dresses cost a bomb. So I went to work. Monday and Thursday evenings and all day Saturday.

I didn't mind. Jobs were more fun than Latin homework. After selling shoes in a crappy chain store on Broadway Avenue for one school year and the summer, I graduated to working as an elevator operator at Fink's, a stylish downtown department store, which boasted four floors of elegant merchandise for ladies. Old Mr. Fink, Senior, had hatched five sons. Each of these sons then floor-walked one of the four levels, haunting the aisles for jumbled displays to put to rights and/or idle salespeople to scold.

The fifth and youngest of the Fink sons was called Wolf. He had gone to Harvard Business and so had been made head executive of the whole works. A master of swagger and suave, when he wasn't locked in his fifth floor office, Wolf Fink ambled about the ground floor aisles ogling the customers and eating peanuts from a small brown paper bag. It was a while before I noticed that he frequently preferred my elevator. I suspected that the main floor lift dispatcher had complained to him about my insubordination and had also revealed that I sometimes intentionally compressed unpleasant shoppers between the doors of my car. I was afraid Mr. Fink would fire me. But I was wrong.

Wolfie Fink was a handsome salt and pepper curly head whose resemblance to Rock Hudson had more than once hit me between the thighs. He was married and the father of some children, but middle age had not yet informed Wolfie that he was nearing forty. He was fit. He played a lot of tennis, squash and golf. He also got plenty of exercise running after women.

One day, Wolfie brought his crumpled paper bag of peanuts into my full lift and stood quietly to the rear of the car. Three ladies got off on Two.

I announced, "Third floor: Ladies dresses. Women's coats. Suits and Casual vacation wear."

The rest of my passengers exited on the third floor.

"Fourth Floor: Furs. Evening wear. Designer Dresses," I called out.

"Five please," his deep voice answered. I wanted to show my prowess at operating his top-of-the-line Otis elevator, but he made me nervous. I lurched us to Five and landed my craft a full inch short of the floor itself. It was, in fact, the first time I had been up this far. Nobody used the fifth floor, except the executives.

We were alone. On Five. Just me and my elevator and Mr. Fink.

Next thing I knew, Wolf placed himself squarely behind me, arms about my waist in the manner of a golf pro. "Just what is a pretty girl like you doing running an elevator?"

"I only work part-time," I mumbled. "I go to school."

"How would you like to be a model? You would sure look cute in those Lanz originals on Three. The pay is better, too." Wolf Fink's licorice-scented Canoe shaving lotion was getting to me. *Did I want to be a model?* What a question. *Did the Virgin Mary want to be the mother of Jesus?*

I squirmed. "I'm afraid I don't have the cleavage for the low-cut dresses," I replied. As I said this, thousands of tiny white heart-shaped Lanz dress buttons mentally dribbled through my fingers. Was I afraid? Or excited? I know I groped for the smooth black penis-shaped elevator handle. My gaze fell upon the elevator inspector's line-by-line monthly signatures: *Chester Wilcowski, Chester Wilcowski, Chester Wilcowski. Where the hell was inspector Wilcowski now that I needed him?*

"I can have the dresses altered to fit you. Or we'll get you some pads for your bra." Wolf was serious. Every single buzzer light on my control panel was lit. Up green and down red arrows flashed urgently before me.

"I'd better get back to the main floor," I murmured. "All the other cars are full. We're busy today."

Was I gasping for breath? Maybe I was. I know I felt shaky. I wanted Wolf to step out on Five so I could express my car all the way back down. It was time for my break. My relief operator would be waiting on One. I could safely hide from Mr. Fink in the employees' basement lunchroom. After my fifteen-minute pause, he'd be gone, I thought. He would be up in the front of the store, chatting with Chris, the platinum blonde leather goods buyer with whom, it was rumored about the store, Wolf had long been having an affair.

Wolf slowly removed his arms from about my sweating self, grazing my boobs as he passed them. "Don't worry about those dash lights flashing," he said. "The dispatcher saw me get into your elevator. Whether I come down with or without you, she won't peep. When is your break?"

"I'm supposed to be on it now. I've already used up five minutes. I only get fifteen," I hurried to say.

"Good. I'll run us down myself and tell Miss Walsh that you are going to take an hour today," said Wolf.

Wolf must have cut his teeth playing with his father's store's elevator controls. He expressed us to the main floor without even stopping to pick up a single agitated customer. I was stuck. Short of kicking Mr. Fink in the shins and blurting the whole business about how the Lion didn't allow me to date Jewish boys, nothing — but nothing — was going to help me now.

Wolf had the relief operator whiz us up to five and invited me into his office for a drink. On his office door was a hand-lettered sign:

"Open Thursday Nites till Nine and All Day Saturday."

"Come on in. I'll show you my paintings." Wolf's office was stacked high with his paintings. Scads of different signs he had handcrafted over the years. Corkboard paneling emblazoned with carefully lettered pasteboards read: Anne Fogarty Fall Trunk Show. John Meyer of Norwich. Special Purchase of Vera Scarves. McMullen Blouses Summer Offer Three Days Only. Adlers Really Stay Up. Hanes Sandal foots Reduced for Clearance. Let Estée Lauder Into Your life. Rings 'n' Things. Everything on the Table $2.00. Harper's Bazaar Says. Authentic Imported Lambswool Pringles Don't Cling. Winter Coats 30% off Regular.'

"You like?" asked Wolfie, gesturing at the rafts of painted boards. My eyebrows said yes. I didn't reply.

"Siddown, siddown, honey. Take a load off. Whaddayou drink?"

The only "drink" drink I had ever imbibed in my life was Seven & Seven and twice I had thrown up right after. "I'll take straight gin. No ice," I said.

Wolf drank Scotch and soda. He fixed himself a double. Then he sat down at his massive carved desk and smiled victoriously. "Well, now, I was about to make you into a model, wasn't I?"

"Really, Mr. Fink, I don't care what job I do. Your store is so neat and with my twenty percent employees' discount, I get by real well."

"I'd like to think of you as one of our fashion models, Miss Hoskins. You have too much class to be an elevator operator. That beige gabardine uniform hangs like a bag on you. Wouldn't you prefer to wear some prettier clothes while you work?" Stepping around to my side of the desk, Wolf gingerly unzipped his fly. I guessed then that he meant business was business.

"Mr. Fink," I spluttered.

"Just call me Wolf." He took short breaths to assure me. "I can give you enough clothes to last your whole life. I looked you up. Your personnel record says you go to Buffalo Seminary. The girls are pretty well dressed up there, aren't they? Couldn't you use a new pair of Spaldings? How about a half dozen cashmere cardigans? You name it, you get it," he said, producing a persuasively firm hard-on.

I blindly stuck my hand out to defend myself and met with the warmth of his generous endowment. The gin tasted exactly like Jean Naté After-Bath Friction lotion and did the nicest things to terror.

58

"I'm a virgin" would be a pretty corny thing to say to a grown man who probably owned three gross of button-down Oxford cloth shirts and had the Buffalo market cornered on Shetland sweaters. I enfolded his thick prick with two hands just to keep it somewhere.

He spoke. "I don't want your virginity, Susan. I was just wondering if you would like to suck me off. Sucking is not dangerous, you know. You just ..." He pushed his cock and my hands right into my face. I had two or three quick thoughts about fleeing the scene, but not one of the escape solutions I came up with included how to tell the Lion I had lost my job. So when I opened my mouth, Fink pushed his dick to the back of my throat and told me to grab him with my lips. I pushed hard at his gray-flannel groin and managed to take a single breath before I told him, "You have to let me take out my retainer, Mr. Fink. It has hooks on it. They're sharp. You'll get cut." His hardened wiener wagging aimlessly, Wolfie backed off. "Wow!" He gasped. "That was a close call. Do you wear that thing all the time?"

My fingers rummaged in my mouth. Drooling, I uttered a toneless "Ummmgghhh," nodded yes, unhooked the hooks and pulled the spit-covered pink plastic retainer apparatus from my mouth. Wolfie handed me a box of Kleenex. I, gaping at his erect pink circumcision, wrapped the retainer in a tissue.

This accomplished, Wolfie again approached my facial area with his weapon. Turning my head sharply to the left, I suggested, "Why don't we just talk for a minute?" Wolfie's dick was smack up against my right ear.

Noting he had missed his target, Wolfie shrank away. "I'm sorry, I thought you were ready," he said, embarrassed.

I righted my head and looked at Wolfie meekly, "Mr. Fink, um ... err ... Sir. I mean ... I guess I'm just inexperienced ... I really don't know how." Wolfie was all tenderness. He knelt down, put both hands on my shoulders and found my eyes. "I really thought ..." he began. "I mean, I expected because you knew about those braces cutting my cock that ..." He caressed my arms gently. "Haven't you ever given anyone a blow job?"

My eyes were wet. Choking on my words I confessed, "I'm not allowed."

"So who's allowed?" Wolfie wondered and shrugged.

I raised my face to his and smiled. "You think I'm silly don't you, sir?" I asked.

Mr. Fink tsked and replied, "Who said anything about silly?"

I worried my retainer out of the wad of paper hanky in my lap, popped it back into the roof of my mouth and explained. "I mean, I'm not sophisticated like you. I'm just a schoolgirl. I'm not up on all these things. I guess ... I guess I'm just dumb."

Wolfie stood up, rocked back on his heels and zipped up. "Look, young lady, I don't know who you think you are coming in here like this all sweetie-pie, lovey-dovey, goody-two shoes and accusing me of thinking you're dumb. I don't think you're dumb or not dumb. I don't exactly check out the IQ of every elevator operator I bring up here for a quickie."

"You might as well fire me, Mr. Fink. I'm only working here to make pocket money. Maybe I'm not your type of girl."

Refilling his own and my glasses with our respective boozes, Wolfie asked me, "Do you still want to be a model?" I sipped my gin and then said, "I wouldn't mind. I love clothes. But I'm such a nerd about this sex thing. I just couldn't begin to learn without knowing you better."

Wolfie's eyes lit up. "Well, then, we'll just have to get to know each other better." He downed his drink, set his empty glass on the desktop, came over and pulled me to my feet. Then he took me in his arms and planted a long, wet kiss on my mouth. As he completed the tonguing of my plastic palate, Wolfie pulled back, patted me on the ass and said, "Meet me downstairs when the store closes. We'll go out for a drink.

Whatever evil still lurked in the Lion's heart in my regard was softened one night when I appeared before him in strapless pale pink tulle and painful whalebone. His baby girl was growing up. He snapped a Polaroid or two.

Although Wolfie Fink was still my part-time lover, on that pink tulle evening, I was going out. On a date. With an Anglo Saxon white person. With a car. I was off to attend a bona fide debutante ball. An uptown, Buffalonian, real estate magnate's daughter was coming out — into Buffalo society. I think my dad hoped I looked "old rich." In reality, I knew I was too skinny, much taller than average, pigeon-toed, knock-kneed, flatter than a pancake and hornier than a shithouse rat.

The deb's mother had chosen my escort, Doug Palmer, because he too was tall. To boot, Doug was thin-lipped, blond, white, pure middle-class, bourgeois, Americana collegiate, golf club Protestant. As we pulled away from the house in Doug's '55 Plymouth, the Lion remarked to a bleating Lamb that if I had to go down the drain, it might as well be with a white guy who had his own transportation. I spent most of that summer in Doug's car. The Lion had made dating rules. "No drive-ins, m'boy," he told Doug. "A nice lad like you wouldn't go to a drive-in anyway, I know. But I have to mention it just so you remember. My daughter Susan is a good girl. I'm sure you get the …

Doug Palmer got the picture, all right. The opening scenes and finales of every drive-in movie he could afford to get blown in were engraved on the backs of his synapses forever. We saw *Friendly Persuasion* and *The Mummy Ghost Returns* seven times each in July and August. During the parts I wasn't getting finger-fucked in, I was either buttoning my Ship n' Shore blouse or pulling up my panties. Doug had probed about in my private parts enough times to know I didn't mind being rubbed between my legs. So he always fiddled my lips and openings while I gave him solid hand jobs or puckered my mouth around his willing throbs till he came.

I, though, never came. Doug was too rapid-fire for that. His manipulations of my tight spot never lasted long nor was he diligent enough in the same spot for any positive result to occur. Doug was a groper. No finesse. A safe white guy from the right suburb whose souse of a father had bought his son a car in hopes he would better be able to keep up with the smarmy set.

Doug did get me home on time and never parked in front of the house for more than the acceptable three minutes. The Lion, picturing his maiden offspring as the belle of country club functions and hops, began to feel grateful she had found herself a reputable boyfriend whose father had money. I galumphed along with the gag, knowing that if we continued to see each other, someday Doug would have to ask for my hand and thereby belong to my future and perhaps, in some vague way, prevent the inevitability of college. By August, I was bored with being pried at and petted in drive-ins, getting worked into a sexual lather and never getting to the finish line. To remedy this, I began asking Doug to run me home as soon as he had fulfilled his needs into his monogrammed hanky. Then, all alone, I would hop between the sheets and open my legs wide. A dollop of Pond's cold cream, and I was once again on my way up and out of the Land of the Band-Aid People.

Exhibiting my pussy by stretching open my thighs, I would then face new crowds of erect gentlemen in my mind and extol the virtues of my private space. "It's tight and wet and snapping good," I told them. Like a princess in a fairy tale, my sweet hole was available to the prince who could prove his valor.

"I can lick you better than any dog," one handsome bloke with a ten-incher promised.

"My fingers are as swift as the wind," said a brown-haired dandy with a peaked cap tipped over one eye.

"Open her up more!" demanded a Big Boss type, whose dick protruded through his half-buttoned fly. "Spread your lips, push out those juices, show us your wet hole, how many of us can you take on?"

I was in my element. Every single man in the netherworld of my mind participated in this flesh auction whilst I brushed and tickled my erect pink button to climax time after time, until I found sleep.

One late night, Doug Palmer's mother phoned the Hoskins house asking for her son. The Lion answered. "Gee, I'm sorry, Mrs. Palmer, but the kids are still at the show. What was it you said you found in your car?"

"A garter belt and stockings which I presume belong to your daughter, Susan," seethed Mrs. P.

"Are you sure of that?" The Lion raised an eyebrow over the receiver at his wife.

"Your daughter wears Hanes seamless sunburst shade number two, doesn't she?"

"Just a moment, please ..." The Lion placed his hand over the mouthpiece and whispered at the Lamb, "Does Susie wear Hanes seamless sunshine shade number two?" My mother shrugged. She hadn't the foggiest.

"Sorry, Mrs. Palmer," said the Lion, "but we aren't sure on our end if she does prefer sunshine number two."

"I did not say sun*shine* number two, "said Doug's mother, "I said sun*burst* number two."

"Just a minute," said the Lion. "Elva," he muttered, "she said burst, not shine."

The Lamb still had no idea.

"Look, Mrs. Palmer, when the kids get back here, I'll ask Susie about the shade on those stockings you found. Okay?"

"No! It's not okay! Where are they? I want my son home this minute. For all we know he's in the back seat with her right now." Mrs. Palmer was in tears.

My dad replied. "Are you insinuating, Mrs. Palmer, that my daughter is corrupting *your* son? Perhaps I should have called *you* long ago. He's the one who's always hanging around our house as though he owned the place. Why he ... he opens our Frigidaire without permission. Even our own kids don't do that."

Mr. Palmer got on the extension then and yelled drunkenly, "Lishen, Mac, I got a deeshent kid. Hish mother's worried about him out with your girl. We lent him our new car yesterday and that kid of yours lef' some o' her underwear in it. If I were you ..."

"If you were me, Mr. Palmer, you would join Alcoholics Anonymous!" The Lion King hung up in their faces.

It was midnight when we kids rolled in.

"Where have you been?" snarled Leo.

"Oh, we went to a movie and then stopped for ice cream at Sully's," I said cheerily, hoping my father didn't know what cum smelled like.

The Lion turned to Doug. "Your behavior, young man, is dis-gusting, criminal even. I could call the police."

Doug was bewildered. "Excuse me, sir, but I ... "

"Your mother phoned here over an hour ago, and five more times since, trying to find you two. She's found some girl's garter belt and stockings in the glove compartment of her new car and claims they belong to Susan. I suggest you explain." The Lion padded about the kitchen table as he spoke.

Doug threw me a jig's-up glance. I scowled at him then laughed out loud. "How silly, Daddy. It wasn't my underpants I left in the car last night, it was just my garter belt and stockings. 'Member, Doug? I got out of the car to go wading."

I winked at Doug and worried about how gray my garter belt must have looked to Doug's tidy mother. I knew I should have listened to the Lamb: no pins in bras and no dingy undergarments. "Wading?" The Lion stopped in his tracks.

"You remember, Dad. Doug took me to Crinny Flickinger's beach party last night. I couldn't go swimming 'cause I've got my little friend, so I just waded. You can't wade in stockings."

The Lion went crimson at the very idea I was having my period and sent me to bed. When I was halfway up the steps, I heard him address the hapless Doug to advise, "You go home now. And paste your father one good. Right in the chops."

CHAPTER SEVEN

B efore he left me at the Buffalo railroad station, the Lion popped me a kiss on the cheek and reminded me, "Remember, Susie, there's no reason for a fellow to buy a cow if he's already getting the milk for free."

I pondered this weighty caution as I settled into my Pullman seat. I thought to myself, *buy the cow?* After a very few minutes, I stopped puzzling about who would be getting whose milk for free and thought about the real miracle. I was being allowed to spend Homecoming Weekend with Doug Palmer at Hamilton College.

Halfway to my destination it dawned on me that the Lion and Doug Palmer must have had a heart-to-heart at my expense. If so, they were in for a shock. Due to imminent bankruptcy — in less than a month's time — the Hoskins family was moving to Chicago. I had private plans to stay on in Buffalo and attend college there, alone. In light of these plans, I had no intention of continuing my relationship with the insipid Doug Palmer beyond the college weekend deflowerment stage. After that, my virginity out of the way, I was determined to go about living my life without benefit of parental — or any other — kind of control.

Doug, awaiting my arrival at the station, had other ideas. He sincerely liked me and my willing juices. Maybe Doug even loved me. I know he wanted to fuck me. So much did Doug desire to penetrate me that he was prepared to offer me his fraternity pin in exchange for my maidenhead. He promised to marry me when we both finished school. Although I wasn't keen, I smiled sweetly and stabbed Doug's frat pin into the lapel of my paisley-print shirt dress.

At Hamilton, dates were housed in the freshman dorms. The boys stayed in their fraternity houses where huge galvanized washtubs were brimful of ice, beer, gin and orange juice.

As I unpacked and readied for the evening's bash, my assigned roommate prattled away while hanging up one quality garment after the other in the closet at the foot of her borrowed dorm cot. Her name was Elizabeth Wells Ramsey, but I could call her Libby. "Don't you think the Hamilton guys are swell?" Libby enthused.

I nodded absently as I watched her from the adjacent bed, awed by the sheer quantity of high-quality plaids, tweeds and houndstooth the rich girl had brought along for a two-day weekend. "Is that cashmere?" I asked, as Libby began folding a pale yellow pullover.

Libby threw the sweater into my lap. "It's a Braemar. I only wear Braemars. They don't pill."

Between my fingers, the cashmere knit felt like softened butter under a silver knife. "It's lovely," I said, returning the sweater to pretty Libby, whose brassy tan looked fresh from a Lake Placid ski run.

With that same epoxied-jaw accent that I had left behind at Seminary, Libby replied, "If you really like it, you may as well have it. It's not my color. Mummy buys them by the dozen at Saks, but I never wear the yellows much." Libby tossed herself stomach-down on the bed. "Seriously," she asked again, "what do you think of these Hamilton guys?"

Crushing the bunny-smooth pullover against my cheek, I admitted, "I only know one Hamilton guy. His name's Doug Palmer. He's my boyfriend from home — sort of. We're from Buffalo."

Libby twirled a lock of her sumptuous hair. "Well, let me tell you, they aren't as randy as the Yalies."

I blushed and said, "I don't know any Yalies. How did you say they were again?"

"Yalies are sex maniacs," she replied. "Hamilton guys have better manners. About sex anyway."

Rolling over on her back, Libby draped her perfect pageboy over the edge of the bed and stared at the ceiling. "All Yale men ever want to do is screw you. I lost mine up there. How about you?"

Redder-faced still, I told Libby the truth. "I'm a virgin."

Libby sat up and clasped her arms around her knees. "Really? Honest to God? How old are you?"

"I'm sixteen," I lied. In fact, I was almost seventeen. But being a virgin at seventeen was retarded.

"Congratulations!" Libby rose and stuck out a perfectly manicured right hand to shake mine. "I was fifteen." She sat down again. "I didn't want it to happen, but there was this boy, you see — good family. Andover, Yale. Three generations. He said he wanted to marry me. So I let him … you know … touch me down there," Libby's

66

voice clouded with regret. She went on, "One night he made me go to a motel with him. I mean he was almost my fiancé. I couldn't very well refuse, could I?"

I murmured. "I guess not."

Libby continued, "His name was Reginald Biddle. I'll never forget that name. It sounds so pure. So Ivy League." Libby seemed to be trying to control an impending sob. "Well, this Reginald guy got me down on the bed at this motel and he ... " she wiped at a tear on her silken cheek, " ... he just whipped it out and raped me right there on the spot." Libby began to cry.

I jumped up and moved to sit by Libby's side. I put my arm around her beige cashmere shoulder to say, "Come on now. It wasn't all that bad, was it?"

Two saddened dish-blue eyes turned to face me. "Don't say that!" she cried. "You don't know how miserable I am. You can't even imagine how awful it is. That cad. That hulking beast of a boor clawing and scratching at me. You don't know what it feels like to wake up the next morning and know that it's gone." Libby shuddered. "Stolen away in the night."

"What exactly happens?" I wished my hair were the color of Libby's. Burnished Radcliffe.

"You want it back," she said, "That's all. You just have this emptiness down there and you want them to give it back. But you can't have it back. It's over. Finished. Done." Libby's wailing became a seething moan between her clenched teeth. "All you can feel is longing. I mean you want to recover what you've lost. An aching hunger seizes you. It's like wanting ... like wanting …"

"A new cashmere sweater?" I tried.

"No, no," Libby sniffled. "It's worse than that. It's existential."

Not sure where Libby was going next, I dropped the subject and began preparing for the evening's festivities.

By eleven o'clock of the first night on campus, I was so sloshed and rattled from a combination of gin and Dixieland that I begged Doug to walk me back to the dorm. I knew that the dorm room coast was clear. Libby had last been seen chug-a-lugging screwdrivers while her date devoured goldfish, straight out of the fraternity house's aquarium.

The cots on which the freshmen slept were comfort approximate. When Doug pushed me down on one of them, the sharp frame's edge shot daggers into my drunken spine. "Down, boy," I told him, as Doug dumped his fully dressed, besotted skin and bones on top of me in the dark.

"Susie," he said. "I love you. You know how mush I love you. I love you sho mush."

He fumbled all over me like a frenzied puppy who desperately needs to find a place to pee. Doug's bony hands were everywhere. I pushed at him and wriggled, trying to edge my lower back off the iron bedrail. But on he rampaged, oblivious to my discomfort. Doug was, as I had been warned, *just after one thing.* To be sure to get this elusive *one thing,* he contorted the fingers of his right hand, the better to get my dress unbuttoned in the back —even though it buttoned all the way up the front.

"It doesn't unbutton there," I said.

Doug responded by taking a second to unzip his gray flannel fly. I seized the opportunity to hike my fanny to midbed and my shirtwaist dress up as high as the physical parameters of metal on one side, wall on the other, would allow. He got busy then yanking my underpants down around my ankles to ensure that his target would be readily available. He shoved one knee between my thighs, "Fantashtic," he slobbered, then he plugged his mouth into mine before I could reply.

Working his prick from his jockey shorts, Doug hand-held the instrument and stabbed at my hairiness. His tongue corked my mouth so firmly that I could only garble my ouches. Doug was not exactly sure where, but he knew that hole must be around there somewhere. And so he continued to thrust his hardened scimitar against the partition between my vagina and my rectum.

I was in seventh hell. My pussy was in an advanced state of alcoholic dehydration and Doug's gray flannel knee was digging great brush burns into my inner thighs. My lower lip was sore from wresting it free of his vacuum-packed kisses. At last, I managed to growl, "Slow down, champ. I'm not resisting you."

Jesus Christ, I thought, *just my luck to end up being devirginized by a virgin.*

To be certain that my sacred deflowering would be achieved then and there, I lifted Doug's stiff pink circumcised lump with my left hand and opened my pussy with my spit-soaked right. I introduced his cock into my gooey secret place and wondered if poor inexperienced Doug might not want me to ejaculate for him as well.

There was some blood. But not a bucketful. After he left, I finished myself off in a hurry. How did I feel? Victorious. Mission accomplished. Next day I took the New York Central RR back to Buffalo. My dad picked me up at the station. "How was it?" he asked.

"Existential," I replied.

CHAPTER EIGHT

I was still seventeen. The remaining Hoskins family was moving from Buffalo to Chicago. The Lion had offered to break both of my legs if I did not give up the idea of staying in Buffalo to attend university there. For Big George it was clear. I should be moving to Chicago with the family. "You can get a good job out there," he told me.

"I want to go to college, Dad," I said.

"What for?" he asked me.

"I want to study languages."

My dad gaped at me. "To study *what?*"

"French," I added, "I ... I would like to study French."

"What the hell can you do with French?" He squinched his eyes, puzzled.

"I want to be an interpreter. You need at least four years of French for that."

"What does an interpreter do?" he said.

"Interprets," I said. "Puts one language into another so the words can be understood by a listener."

"Susie, you're a girl. Girls get married. They can't go flying off somewhere to interpret foreign languages. Who will take care of their kids? Who will feed their husband? Look at your sister Sally. She was in college for two years. Then she dropped out and got married. Now she has a baby. She can't go get a job. She's busy being a housewife. Do you think your own mother would want to get a job? Of course not. It's normal. Anyway, you can't stay in Buffalo on your own. You'll be all alone."

"Dad," I said, "I feel good when I'm all alone. I am not afraid to take the bus at night or go to a bar by myself. I like being able to make my own hours and my own decisions."

The Lion paled and shook his handsome balding head again. "Susie," he pleaded, "can't you just be normal?"

I laid my hand gently on my dad's forearm and said, "No, Daddy. I can't. Normal just doesn't work for me."

My father was crestfallen. He frowned a dark gray frown. I was rejecting him. I knew it. And I was sorry. Nonetheless, I had endured my fill of parental guidance. I sincerely wanted to carry on alone.

"All right, Susie," my dad said. "Go ahead. Go to your damn college in Buffalo. But if you do that, you'll be paying your own way."

State Teachers College was cheap: Fifty dollars a semester. I could manage it. Moreover, in order to help me pay school fees, Wolfie Fink had agreed I might work a couple of extra nights a week at the store. After the doors closed at nine, I was Wolfie's own private mannequin.

Over the past two years, Wolf Fink had become quite a mouthful. He was my patron. I didn't have a boyfriend yet. So Wolfie was my boyfriend pro tem. Under his tutelage, I had learned to be a smashing floor model. I had also dispensed with my unbecoming orthodontics altogether and gave him deliriously good head. Following a dull day over the drawing table and in between Scotches, nothing pleased Wolfie more than to ring up the junior dress department and whistle for me to come up for a preview showing in his newly decorated office.

He had done the place over for me. I wanted green wallpaper with rosebuds all over it. But even I could see that rosebuds wouldn't work for a man's office.

Wolf did, however, adopt my favorite shade of limey green for the walls. I had also asked him to put in white couches and lots of hanging planters full of ferns and ivy. Wolfie ordered the new furniture and hired a gardener to come in and care for the greenery every week. We were getting to know each other.

And I, by now, was dressed to my straightened teeth. I paraded high fashion from the ground floor hosiery department to the elegant designer dress floor at Fink's. Grateful to be off my feet for an hour, I answered the Wolf's whistles cheerfully. Sucking his cock was the least I could do in return for his generosity, and besides, I had learned to like gin. Straight with rocks. Drinking gin was like drinking perfume. Wolf's prick always wore a hard smile on the end. Sitting in his big swivel chair — I on my knees between his open legs with my face in his lap — he ruffled my hair and bantered sexily while I worked.

"Your lips are so smooth around my dick. That's it, baby, run your tongue around the tip. Harder, softer, right there. That's it. Stay there now and press on that spot. Now suck me deep. Take it all in, right up to the hilt. That's it. Move your head up and down. Ohhh, honey, you're too good to me. No, no don't stop. I love it. Feel how much harder it gets? Do you feel it in your cunt? I bet your cunt is wet and hot now. I wish I could push myself inside. This is too good. Don't worry. That's it. Keep sucking. I—I'm going to come soon … Stop a second. Wait. Take a break."

Wolf always kept my glass of straight gin handy on the desk and lowered it to moisten my lips during the rest periods. It was true, my undies grew sopping moist during these sessions and I worried I might sully a Jonathan Logan shift or damage an expensive Suzy Perette frock. I also hankered to put my hand in my pants and find my own little gadget during these sessions. But I knew that Wolfie would never understand. He still thought I was a total virgin, saving myself for the right man who would be my husband.

Wolfie was a tender master, caressing my hair and calling me "baby" and "honey" the way he did. He didn't have to do that. I really didn't mind taking his thing in my mouth. In fact, it felt pretty good. He was a clean man. Not ugly or sweaty or even fat. He played sports and had a very pretty wife. Once I got the hang of curling my lips back over my teeth so I wouldn't scratch him with my incisors, I enjoyed this extracurricular activity almost as much as he did.

To be sure, there had been an apprenticeship. At first, my cheek muscles got sore every five seconds, but I had practiced on my own in the bathtub. Sucking in my cheeks, then ballooning them and holding it as long as I could. Sticking the shampoo bottle down my throat as far as I could without gagging. It was merely a question of calisthenics — mind over matter. People only retched on cum and gagged on big pricks because they didn't have enough practice.

After a few turgid college months living in a furnished room with neighbors in South Buffalo, I had moved uptown into a dingy third-floor garret with the only man at school who, amid the married vets and vapid fraternity jocks, made any sense. His name was Roderick Post. Rod was an art student and came from upper state and lower class. He painted abstracts and loved purity, sweetness and innocent sweet young things like me. Had he known that his own ingénue/prodigy/protégée was busily burning her candor at both ends — well, he did not know and for the moment, it was better that way.

I had fallen in love with Rod in an elective drama class. At first, I found him standoffish. But he was merely being charismatic. His very reserve made him sexy. In that drama class, Rod persisted in sending me cryptic notes laden with flowery prose about my "Knice Knees" and "Lollipop Legs." It wasn't much, but it was more amorous attention from someone close to my own age than I was used to. Besides, Rod's feathery long eyelashes were attached to sleepy bedroom lids, and his top lip curled unilaterally when his syrupy voice revealed the unimaginable wealth of subjects he knew a lot about: Picasso, Kant and Allen Ginsberg were Rod's familiars. He had few dress-up clothes, but he possessed a wealth of coffee table art books. Dali, Braque and Matisse volumes littered the table in front of his tattered old couch. Rod was not chic. But he was smart. I liked smart. Rod had a clever method of procuring his expensive art books. It involved joining a book club that offered free books. You ordered. The books arrived. You could keep them for a certain length of time. If you didn't like them after a specific date, you had to send them back. Rod kept his. They billed him and bullied him. He never paid. Then he would join the same club under a new name and receive the next stock of art books he so coveted but couldn't pay for. For me, Rod was a bottomless source of shrewd tricks and cultural knowledge. He had the brand of smarts that I coveted. He also valiantly protested all manner of injustice and had dreams of living in a better world where artists were supported by the government and supplied housing with skylights and studios.

Rod was not classically handsome. He was medium tall, angular and gaunt. His skinny nose pointed downward and he slouched. His face was acne- pitted. I didn't mind how he looked because his serenely mysterious, hyper- intellectual presence never clunked, clattered or banged. In the hip language of my future, Rod would have been thought of as "cool." What culture- hungry young woman would not have fallen in love with a brilliant, cool, abstract painter in 1957?

While I lay awake in the old iron bed that came with the furnished garret, I often wondered how someone as delicately sensitive to beauty as Roderick Post could accept living in such a hovel. The paint on the walls of the two tiny rooms under the eaves was chipped and had long since lost its color. In the kitchen, a spotted green claw-foot gas range provided both central heating and cooking privileges. There was no refrigerator and no kitchen sink; the dishes had to be washed in the tiny bathroom's basin. The place wouldn't have passed inspection with either the health department or my parents, who still thought I was living with a girlfriend on Elmwood Avenue at Potomac Street, in order to be closer to school.

Rod was nineteen. He claimed to have had some experience with women and was pleased when I assured him I'd had none with men. I had to lie. Rod had made it clear that he thought a woman should remain pure until she married. This attitude was based on the teachings of medieval scholars whose works lined the brick-and-board bookshelves along Rod's bedroom walls. He promised to teach me all about history and culture, art and drama, books and music. Those promises melted my heart.

For the first month we lived together, I slept chaste beside my strange friend. Though Rod would often request that I touch his cock or simply sit and watch while he gave himself a handful, he never attempted to have his way with me or compromise my virginity. For him, the important thing about a romance between boy and girl was culture. As a couple we often went out to view exotic French films, visit art galleries or listen to free concerts of baroque music. In return for his teaching me about the artsy side of life, I copied The Lamb. I was Little Susie Housekeeper. I made Rod a good hearty supper each evening, kept his clothes clean and sat quietly reading at the kitchen table whenever his Bohemian friends came calling. Sometimes these types stayed on until the smallest hours, gabbling with Rod about the esthetic process, arguing the value of creativity in the twentieth century or making sweeping decisions regarding the responsibility of government to subsidize painters no matter how much or how little work they might produce.

For me, their speeches were exciting news. The beat poets — Allen Ginsberg, Lawrence Ferlinghetti, Gregory Corso and Philip Lamantia — -, Rod informed me, were national heroes. I read them. But failed to comprehend them. Even if Henry Miller was the real messiah and James Joyce, by virtue of his sheer incomprehensibility, was a noble persecuted genius and Pete Seeger was God, I privately considered

74

there would never be an artist more fascinating and marvelous than my very own Roderick Post.

Eventually Rod got around to committing the act of sex with me. Did I seduce him? Yes. I suppose I did. I rubbed my legs on his a lot and caressed his fanny till, finally, he gave in. To my dismay, our first and all subsequent fucks were humdrum chores. If, as he had assured me, Rod was experienced with women, you couldn't have proved it by me. Mind you, he had taken to our new game with admirable vigor. But Rod was a hopper-on and a hopper-off. A putter-in and a taker-out. He was more a gymnast than a lover.

In those days, I didn't mind. Screwing had its charms. There was the contact of Rod's spindly, nude body against mine. And sometimes there even occurred a bit of billing and cooing before. And, by now, the penetration part was neither painful nor terrific; it was just sort of *there*. Once in a while, in certain positions, I felt light squiggles in my thighs as Rod humped away over me. But these hints of sensation were nothing — God forbid — to write home about.

What did cause some wakefulness for me was an entirely new type of anxiety. A panic really.What would happen if I got venereal warts, crabs, clap, pregnant, or even an honorable discharge? To whom could I go? All the doctors I knew were our own pediatricians and family practitioners. They would surely feel duty-bound to tell my father that I was both living with a man and having intercourse.

The very thought of what scathing reproaches and eventual punishment would result from such a news leak almost made me wish I didn't have a boyfriend at all. Nonetheless, you had to have a fellow. Everyone had a boyfriend. Everyone went steady with someone else. To me, it was confusing. The act of love itself could ruin a girl's life, and yet, in my college days, if you didn't have that special Valentine sweetheart, you might as well have been ugly and fat.

I asked the advice of an older woman at school who advised me to go to Planned Parenthood. I did that and was quite matter-of-factly — no questions asked — fitted for a diaphragm. I continued to allow Rod to grind away at me most every night. Although I felt absolutely no twinge when he performed these ritual couplings, I told myself that it was my own fault. I had managed to destroy all of my vaginal taste buds by rubbing and fingering my clitoris so much. If I had known at the age of ten what I knew now, I would never have let my hand venture anywhere near my pussy.

So while Rod was engaging my most private parts in his interminable push-me pull-yous, I counted the faded peonies on the bedroom ceiling. Then, as he neared climax, I would force out a few guttural groans, wiggle my fanny like crazy and cry "I love you" as many times as fit the occasion.

When Rod took me home to his small upstate town for Christmas vacation, his parents treated me royally. When I took Rod with me to Chicago the next Christmas, the Lion treated him like a North Korean. My dad, back on his financial feet, had begun a new list of the minorities that a young woman ought to avoid. These included: actors, writers, painters, circus performers, dancers, musicians and poets who not only had questionable morals but most of them were *faggots*. Regardless of creed or pocketbook, they were included on the Lion's updated shit list. After the holidays, he wrote me a letter to explain that I must cease going out with "that painter guy" because it was a well-known fact that all artists kill their wives. In other words, my Dad was sure that Rod was not only a homosexual, but that he would one day run me through with a paintbrush.

When, months later, I had not accepted my father's order to break up with Rod, he appeared on our doorstep. Rod, being a gentle sort, opened the door and greeted the slightly paunchy Lion, "Hello, Mr. Hoskins. How nice to see you."

"Keep your grubby hands off my daughter or I will kick your rotten teeth down your throat!" said my father.

This comment was met with much aplomb by Rod, who retorted, "Why don't you get a grip on yourself, Mr. Hoskins, and lose some weight?" Rod then closed the door in my father's face.

Next day, I came face to face with my dad as he descended the stairs of the college administration building. He looked cross. And glum.

I spoke right up. "Daddy, what are you doing here?"

"I came to take you out of school," he said.

"You mean you drove here to Buffalo all the way from Chicago so you could take me out of college?"

"That's right, Susie," he said. "I want you to come home."

"But Dad I'm ..." I started.

"I know. I met with the dean. You're eighteen. You're not a minor. I can't take you out of school. It's too late," he muttered.

I felt rather sorry for my poor old dad. I knew he was trying to protect me. To lighten his load, I said, "Maybe you can't take me out of school. But can you take me out to lunch?"

He smiled and asked me where I wanted to go. I said, "Cole's on Elmwood. It's not far. We can walk."

After lunch, my dad went off to visit some old friends from South Buffalo. I went back to classes.

Next day, my father drove his disappointment back to Chicago, and I decided to rearrange my life. From now on, I would be Rod's property. His girl. I began this overhaul by giving Wolfie Fink a farewell blow job.

"Sorry, Wolf, I can't work here and be your girl anymore. I'm committed." To make up the difference in my income I took a part-time job as a French tutor, settled down to cleaning Rod's apartment, cooking and vowing to be faithful to my genius painter forevermore.

In my new role, I always shut up and sat still whilst Rod talked. I was the mistress of a sensitive artist. So sensitive, in fact, that all he wanted to do was daub paint on canvas. One canvas. The same one canvas that for the past two years had served him so well. Rod sincerely did not care if anyone ever saw his artwork. He envisioned a prosperous future wherein I would have a job as a teacher which would keep him in sable brushes for life, thereby permitting his expression to remain forever abstract.

From where I sat then, I fancied this scenario. I would get to be the wife of a brilliant artist. I would encourage Rod and make him want to be famous.

All went well until the middle of senior year when I felt oddly horny. Usually, after every barren coition with Rod, I discreetly finished myself off in the tiny bathroom. Now Rod's hard-ons had abruptly dropped off. I would have to discuss this with him.

I cut two classes, bought a three-dollar pork roast and a bottle of cheap red. I placed a candle on the table and set the scene for an evening's worth of truth game. I put the meat in the oven at five. It would be well caramelized by the time he came in at seven.

Seven-thirty came and went. Then eight on the dot became eight forty-five. By nine-thirty I was alternately livid and worried. Rod might have been in an accident. No. It was probably nothing. Just out with the boys for a few beers. I saved the roast.

Ten-thirty going on eleven. Still no Rod. I allowed myself alternate bouts of anger and fret. *Goddamn him anyway.* Then I begged God to make him all right. I could have gone down and used the landlady's phone. Called the police. No, Rod hated cops. I tried to concentrate on Nathanael West's funniest story and didn't succeed. *Where the hell was Rod?*

At midnight, Rod came in. He sat at the kitchen table and hung his head.

"My God! I had you lying in a snow bank frozen solid," I gasped. It was annoying. He appeared undamaged.

"Are you angry?" Rod looked up. But he did not look at me.

"A little, I guess. But I'm glad you're okay. I feel better already."

"Do you know where I've been?" Rod stared straight ahead.

"No. And I don't really care. I'm fine now that you're home. Want some cold roast pork? There's a nice crunchy end bit. Want me to heat it up?" I was busying myself, electing not to hear what I feared most: another woman.

"Just sit down for a minute," said Rod. "I'm not hungry. I'm glad you waited up. Gotta talk to you." His lips quivered. Rod was pale as death under his acne.

I sat. "You don't have to say where you went," I said. *What would I do if he threw me out?*

"Susie, I'm tired of hiding this from you. I have to tell you before …"

"Look, Rod honey, let's just forget it? You go out whenever you like. I'll always be here when you get home. I'll make you some tea." I got up and fumbled for the kettle.

"Please stay close to me. Don't leave me now." Rod held his head in his hands.

"I'm not going anywhere. I mean it. I love you. Even if there's somebody else. I'll stick by you."

Rod moaned through sonorous sobs. "Susie, you have to help me. I'm sick. I must be sick. Maybe I'm crazy. Or perverted. I've never told anyone. Nobody. Ever."

I sat back down. *What the heck?*

His hands still partially covering swollen red eyes, Rod went on, "It's like I can't help it. I can't keep from doing it."

What could he mean? Shoplifting? Drinking? Pinching tiny Paul Klees from the Albright Art Gallery?

He spoke. "I … what I do is I go someplace where nobody knows me. A suburb or a bus station. Then I just … well ... I ... I expose myself to people. I take it right out and show it to them." A very graphic hand movement made the story come alive. "And Susie, I can't help it."

"You mean exposing yourself like …?"

"Yes, that's right. Like those dirty old creeps who used to scare you in the park when you were a little girl."

"But why? Why ever would you want to do that?"

"I don't know. How am I supposed to know why? It's just there. I'm not a psychiatrist for Chrissake."

Rod was losing his temper. That was healthy. Only this morning my psychology instructor had told the whole class, "Anger is sanity." Rod was coming around. His confessions, however, did not reassure me. Being locked in an attic apartment with a sex pervert was not my idea of your average desirable sexual fantasy.

"Well, maybe you should tell me how it manifests." The Laws of Human Dynamics, Chapter one — Jargon.

"Yes, yes, I can do that." Now his eyes blazed with excitement and my drawers soaked with alarm. "I feel depressed for four or five days. Nervous. Irritable — you know how I get. Then I feel it tempting me. Not all the time. Just if I'm alone or bored in class or something. I get this image of myself doing it, like a snapshot in my head."

"And then?" Even certifiably bananas, I loved him.

"Well, I fend it off and tell it to go away. That works for a couple more days. Then one day when I'm supposed to be somewhere else, I'm just not there. I'm on a bus or in a park or some housing develop-ment, displaying my penis to the sexiest twelve-year-old girl I can

79

find. While I'm doing it, it's not really me doing it, if you get what I mean. It's like watching myself on TV."

"But it is you, isn't it?"

"Yeah, it's me all right. It's like a game. My team is the boys and their team is the girls. The boys have to get a lot of points. More even than the girls, because they're only girls. It's like a handicap. You know, like bowling."

I nodded.

"While I'm hunting for the right girl to show it to, I hear the referee in my head calling out penalties for our side and the scorekeeper racking up points for them. I have to help my side. I have to hurry and make us a point before time's up. So as soon as I find the prettiest, most innocent kid of all, I have this really big hard-on. Then, I just unzip my fly and pull it out before the referee calls time. And we win!"

I gaped, stupefied. "And what does the girl do? Does she scream and run away?"

"No, of course not. She loses the game."

Maybe all artists did kill their wives.

CHAPTER NINE

I t was all set. For our last year of college, Rod would be treated by a group of state-provided psychiatrists at City Hospital. His disorder would be the subject of in-depth therapy, round-table discussions and coffee hours for interns. I had always thought of myself as relatively unhinged, but as Rod suffered from a more drastic pathology, for the time being, my own bats could remain safely cloistered in their belfry.

The frequent outpatient visits exhausted Rod. And I had all I could do to keep up with schoolwork and our wedding preparations. June would be a busy month. Graduation and marriage on the same day. Rod helped me pick out a gorgeous hobble-skirted off-white crepe. And Wolfie Fink offered it to me as a wedding present. The Gypsy gave a shower and invited old Hoskins family friends who came to decorate my new life with acres of yellow-striped percale Springmaid sheets, hand-crocheted his-and-hers house slippers, satin guest towels, too many spice racks, electric mixers, knife sharpeners, can openers, clock radios, irons and whistling tea kettles.

Rod claimed he still liked my body. But he just never felt much like screwing anymore. I felt more like it than ever. I suppose, in a way, I didn't mind that Rod had ceased slamming away every day. To tide me over until I was properly married, housed and employed, I located images upon which I had not yet pounced in my earlier peregrinations. When Rod went to his appointments, I, the bride-to-be, indulged in strictly ephemeral infidelities. Physical betrayal of the ailing Rod with real men never entered my thoughts.

In bed with myself, I became a freak call girl. Spreading my legs and drawing them up high, I put my hand to the task of preparing my cunt for cocks no other girl could take on. For clitoral support, there was a gentle nonentity named Jim, who stood by as my protector and stage manager. Jim had an average-size organ and a motorized finger with which he stroked me to erection before even allowing the customer to enter the room. Sometimes Jim talked of sucking or licking my clitoris, but he never actually got around to it because his head would have gotten in the way of the rest of the story.

In this fantasy, as in some others, I lay on a hard white table. Jim wore clothes. I did not. He caressed my breasts, massaged my clitoris and presented his case. "There's this guy out there who wants to fuck you. He's willing to pay a lot. Got a giant dick. He's been searching for someone who can take him on."

"How big is he?"

"He says nine, but I'd say almost twelve. He's thick, too. Maybe three inches in diameter. You think you can handle that?"

Petting madly at myself, I spoke up. "Well, that guy the other day had a really big one and I did all right, didn't I?"

"You mean that big blond guy? Yeah, he really had a hunk of meat on him. Sure. You did great."

"Did you ask for a hundred dollars?"

"Oh, he'll pay full price. He's desperate. I'm warning you, he's huge."

"I'll take a look at it. Ask him to come in and show it to me." At this point my index finger would be going like sixty on alternate sides of my clitoris.

"Okay, Susie, but I don't think he's going to like that. He's worried that if you see his huge cock, you'll refuse him. I tell you the guy's in a bad way."

Jim always managed to persuade our clients to come and speak to me pre-fuck. Usually the client was a well-dressed white-collar worker. "Good afternoon, Miss. Jim here tells me you don't want to let me fuck you."

A needy case. Lacking self-confidence. Poor rejected spirit. I alone could help him out.

"I'd like to take a look at your penis. I think I can accommodate you, but I must see you first. Frankly, I have handled so many men like you without undue discomfort I can hardly imagine ... is yours merely a problem of size?"

"Well, you see, I have a very unwieldy cock. Women always refuse to let me enter them. My wife took one look on our wedding night and flew the coop. Haven't seen her since. Whores turn away in disgust. The only relief I ever get is with great big floppy holes that aren't any fun. I want some tight cunt. Jim tells me you're the girl for me. He claims you like the biggies."

At this point Jim always resumed his tableside position and manned the diddles so that I might mentally unzip the gentleman's fly and proceed with my examination of his member. As a rule, the men protested. But I knew how to calm them with gentle pish-tushes and don't-you-worries. "Just one little peek." And out I would pull a real salami of a hard-on.

The man blushed and excused himself all over the place. "I'm sorry miss. I know it's just too big. It's all right if you say no. I'm used to being rebuffed."

"Now, now. It's lovely. As Jim probably told you, I adore large cocks. Yours is very big — perhaps the fattest I have ever seen. But never you mind, we'll arrange something."

I turned to my assistant. "Jim, will you spread my cunt more, please. We shall have to proceed slowly. Open me up all the way now."

"Should I put the straps on your legs?"

"No, no. I think I can keep them open if you just hold the lips wide so our friend here can stick it in. Keep your hand going, now. Mustn't let me dry out."

The fantasy gentleman caller was interested in Jim's role. He knew nothing of clits. "You mean he gets to keep his finger on your pussy while I fuck you?"

"Oh, yes, of course. Didn't he explain? Just as you have your little problems with women, I have mine with men. I have to be touched or rubbed to make me come. All my sensations come from that. No matter the size or shape of a man's cock, although it feels good inside me, it can't make me climax. Jim tells me it's because I masturbated so much as a child. He knows because his thing is all bent from jerking off in a dresser drawer. In fact, if it weren't for Jim's talent at making me come just as you enter me, we wouldn't even be here. We specialize in the Cum Cunt Technique."

Promptly then, I would press on my thickened clitoris to hurry it to orgasm. After coming, the warm buzzings in my ears never lasted more than a few minutes. In a matter of seconds, I would be on my feet starting dinner or going over lesson plans for practice teaching.

By the week before commencement, both Hustle and Bustle had moved in on me. The Unitarian minister from the church at Elmwood and West Ferry had agreed to marry us. Rod had asked for a week's grace from the doctors for a short honeymoon in the Thousand Islands.

The Buffalo Board of Education had agreed to give me a $3,900 salary plus a bonus for lunch monitoring as of September. I would be teaching sixth grade at PS 45.

The angry Lion wrote about my wedding, "Your mother spends all her time crying over you. I can't concentrate on my work. If you had an ounce of sense, you would leave that fairy at the altar. A jilt is better than a jolt!" Rod's parents dropped us a line wishing us lifelong luck and sorry they could not attend the ceremony.

I was ecstatic. Still over the moon in love with and in awe of my future mate. He had so much to offer. Whoever would have imagined I might marry a painter? Maybe one day he would become famous. We could go to Europe or appear on television!

Mrs. Roderick Post cordially invites you to attend a one-canvas show of her husband's latest work. We could charge four thousand dollars for that one canvas. We would be rich and popular and ever so attractive. But I knew that fame would not spoil me. I even warned Rod, "We have to be very careful not to get snooty. Even though we are so special and different, we'll keep the common touch. Isn't that right, darling?"

Rod had been in bed for three days. Wan against the already twice-laundered yellow shower-gift sheets, he lay there mumbling to himself.

I, folding laundry at his bedside, prattled on without listening, "...And we will always give lovely parties and invite old friends. Even if we make lots of money. We will always remember our old friends."

Rod pulled on the towel in my hand, saying, "Susie, my doctor wants to see you. Everything is a mess. I'm sorry."

"I'll call him right after we get home from our trip." I flattened the last comer on a flowered pillowcase. "Dr.Webster has really helped you, hasn't he, darling?"

Rod sat up. "Susan," he said, "I'm talking to you. I said the doctor wants to see you. He doesn't want me to get married."

"He doesn't what?"

"I said the doctor has to see you. He says we should think it over."

"Think what over?"

"The wedding," Rod supplied.

84

I knew in my heart of hearts that once we were legal there would be no more talk of mental disturbance, no further need for Rod to carry on his covert street games. As his wife, I would have clout with Rod. I would make life so delectable for him at home, he would never have the urge to flash again.

"Rod, my poor darling," I said, using my uppity teacher tone, "Dr. Webster is not God. He's a public servant. A mere state employee. Objectively, can you possibly think he knows what is best for you? Why, he's practically a perfect stranger. Shall we just leave him out of this? Next year we'll find you a good private man. Meanwhile, why not just leave the important decisions up to me?"

Rod looked frightened. "All I know, Susie, is that I'm not getting married until the doctor says I can. It's too risky." He picked at some errant green caterpillars on the chenille bedspread.

"I swear, if that dumb doctor told you to paint goat vomit on your English muffins every morning before drinking a cup of Abyssinian cat pee, you would obey him. All right, I'll see him. But I'm warning you, I intend to give him a piece of my mind!"

I knew peanuts about psychiatry, but I did know I was not about to make a fool of myself in front of a Unitarian minister. To make that very clear, early next morning I accompanied Rod to the hospital's psychiatric unit.

The city hospital waiting room was cold. The beige-on-beige Formica-topped tables still bore clean ashtrays. Freshly starched nurses squeaked to and fro on crepe soles, oblivious to our presence. Spent magazines with all their recipes, sexy cartoons and coupons for ordering various items long since ripped out by visitors lay stacked in neat piles awaiting the beginning of the hospital day.

"Miss Hoskins?" Dr. Webster stepped out and beckoned me enter.

"Shall I come in, too?" Rod inquired.

"Not yet, Mr. Post. We'll call you."

Five enormous heads wearing glasses and white jackets sat staring at me from around a conference table that appeared to be six feet off the floor and buried under reams of file folders. The door closed behind me. I took a seat.

My breakfast wanted out in all directions at once. It settled for seeping out through my pores. I was sweating puddles. Worse still, in times of tragedy and tension, I had a bad habit of giggling to myself.

"Okay, you guys," I told my bravest self. "Lemme have it. Put 'er there. Sock a homer, baby, and right over that plate. I can take it. Don't worry, gentlemen, they don't call me *The Rock* fer nothin'. I'm a tough customer. Go ahead. Tell it like it is. My future husband is an incurable flasher-painter-wife-beater-incipient-murderer-hanging-wiener-wagger. Go ahead. Inform me that flashing is a terminal illness." Out of breath inside my head, I waited, mute, for the verdict.

"Miss Hoskins," one of the five men said.

"Please, just call me Susan." Humble, keep it humble.

I felt their gazes smacking first my right cheek, then the left. The voices of authority pummeled me from within. Why did I always have to act so tough? So smart-assed? So bold? So in love? I bit a hangnail.

"Your fiancé is a very sick man. His is not a simple problem. He has been diagnosed as an exhibitionist." Pause.

Couldn't that doctor have said flasher? Nobody said exhibitionist in real life, did they? I toyed with the idea of acting shocked, but they knew that I knew that they knew that I knew. So feigning ignorance was out. "I am aware of that." Nod, shift, cross ankles primly under table and sit up like a lady.

"Susan," said a handsome doctor with a continental accent. "We haff made significant progress with Rod. He iss trying to cooperate with us. But ... well . . . you must postpone the marriage. Rod is not up to it. Not ready." Calculated stop.

I had thought Rod was as ready as I was. His mother had sent him money she'd saved up from her meager house allowance so he could buy a wedding suit and a pair of cordovan wingtip shoes. He seemed ready to me.

I was so nervous, I pushed my middle finger all the way into my mouth and sucked hard before popping it out to ask wetly, "W...why do you say he is not ready?"

"Marriage at this time would place too much strain on Rod. His mind is fraught with incomprehensible images. He lives with hostilities perhaps even we do not fully understand. He seems to have gained some control over his desire to expose himself. But the excessive promiscuity has us baffled. In time, we may be able to..."

Prom is cuity? It took me a few seconds to get my ears around the word. I gaped, thunderstruck.

"I suppose Rod has also told you about all the women." The doctor in charge now wore the self-satisfied smirk of someone who has just let a horde of pumas out of a very small calico sack in a jammed elevator.

In a matter of seconds, my face was burning with a combination of rage and shame. I realized all of a sudden that I had been playing Madame *Stay-At-Home-Beat-Your-Beaver* with Jim and the biggies whilst Rod was out ravishing our fair city's female population. Emptying his misery out the blunt end of his tortured soul and into the pussies of our town's Doloreses and Barbaras and Janices and — *Jesus, Mary and Joseph! What next?* "No, Doctor, he never told me," I choked out.

"Now, don't be too hard on yourself, Miss Hoskins. You're in love with Rod. He knows that. He loves you, too. His need for variety in his sex life, difficult though it may be to remedy, has a rather simple explanation. Rod has fixated on you as a mother figure. His impotence in your regard stems from that fixation. The immediate task is to stop him from exposing himself. We must be allowed to help him before he gets caught."

Caught? *Holy shit. Maybe the nice doctor man is right. What if they nabbed him? Picked him up?* Sirens, police, ladies shrieking, "Filthy pig! Masher! Pervert! Yes, officer, it's him all right. I'd recognize that wiener anywhere."

I was crying now. Blubbering noisily right in front of the board of experts. Rampant images pranced through my mind. A desk sergeant phoning me at three in the morning to say that my hubby's in the clink with his pants down and could I get over there right away with a few thousand dollars and a lawyer?

I fancied seeing the Sunday Rotogravure section of the Buffalo Evening News featuring Rod exhibiting sneaky flashing techniques to watch for in your neighborhood these days. All the twelve-year-old girls on all the buses and in all the parks and museum ladies' rooms all over Western New York testifying in court, pointing accusations at the man Susie Hoskins had married because she was so damned sure that all artists didn't kill their wives.

When we called off the wedding, Rod's mother, Mrs. Post, was more than disappointed. She was despondent. She had so counted on her firstborn son marrying and hatching some grandkids for her to love and hug and babysit. Caring for babies would have taken her mind off the terrible facts of her own marriage. You see, her hardworking fireman husband had long been having an affair with Mrs. Post's own classy, widowed mother.

A severe clinical depression inched in and took over her mind. Poor Mrs. Post was reduced to a zombie housewife again. Then one fine day she fashioned herself a see-through hood out of seven layers of Saran Wrap and took to her bed. Rod got to wear his wedding suit and cordovan wingtips — to his dear mother's funeral.

As for me, that September I moved to New York City where I landed a last- minute job teaching French on Long Island. That year, I lived in Manhattan in a dirty great walkup on East 41st Street with a fellow teacher. We reverse commuted in a used Dodge car I had bought on credit. Did I know how to drive? Yes. Did I know how to teach French? Not really. But I would learn.

New York is the only city I have ever lived in that gave me claustrophobia. Everyone I met in New York was currently seeing or was employed as an analyst, a therapist, a psychiatrist, a psychologist or a shrink. After one school year, I simply had to get out of there. So I skedaddled. I grabbed the first teachers association charter flight to Paris.

PART TWO
PARIS

I'm as restless as a willow in a windstorm
I'm as jumpy as puppet on string
I'd say that I have spring fever
But it isn't even spring
I am starry eyed and gravely discontented
Like a nightingale without a song to sing
Oh why should I have spring fever?
When it isn't even spring?

I keep wishing I were somewhere else
Walking down a strange new street
Hearing words that I have never heard
From a man I've yet to meet...

But I feel so gay

In a melancholy way

That it might as well be spring

CHAPTER TEN

It was late June 1961. I was twenty-two. And tingling. The very air of Paris set me alight. I shone — like a skinny Christmas tree. I was still too tall. Too defiant. Too unladylike. Too daring. Too silly. Too mouthy. But I didn't speak French well enough to be *too damned smart for my own good.* That part needed work.

I had arrived in gracious, sprawling, feminine Paris after one year in manly, right-angle, erector-set New York City. Although I knew next to nothing about her, I was enchanted by the City of Light.

As I ascended the stairs at the St. Michel Métro station, lugging more than half my weight in a black and red plaid canvas valise, Lady Paris tendered me a rich *Bonjour.*

The Boulevard St. Michel slanted its wide sidewalks upward, revealing three or four cross streets lined with two-dollar-a-night hotels. I had chosen to stay in the Latin Quarter. I had found it on the map of Paris in Frommer's *Europe on Five Dollars a Day.* I dragged my leaden suitcase and bright blue plastic flight bag, slung over a slippery shoulder, southward up the hill until I found *la rue des Écoles.* Stopping on the corner of this, the street of the schools, I sat myself down in an outdoor wicker chair on the crowded terrace of *Le Café Select Latin,* secured my baggage to me with the strap of my purse and consulted my guidebook.

"Mademoiselle?" came a voice from over my head. I looked up, squinted against the late afternoon glare and saw a mustachioed, heel-clicking French waiter in a black vest and white apron. He was bearing a loaded tray upon his shoulder. *"Mademoiselle?"* he repeated.

As yet too shy to attempt my schoolgirl French, I smiled, saying, "Coke?" According to my guidebook, Coca-Cola was the only international drink guaranteed not to give you diarrhea. The waiter pirouetted away from me and hollered into the bar, *"Un Coca!"*

In a Paris minute, which lasts about three minutes, a familiar greenish squat bottle of Coke was placed on the table before me. It was accompanied by an empty glass, a thin round of sliced lemon and a spoon — all three sitting on a saucer. Underneath all this was wedged a cash register receipt on which the figure "1.80" was underscored by a message in large blue letters, *SERVICE COMPRIS.* No tip necessary? I wasn't sure.

I had been in Paris for exactly one hour, and thus far had tried out my lamentable repertoire of recommended tourist cues on a number of life situations. None of them had worked. I had memorized the tourist chart of new francs on the plane. But French money was painted with multicolored pictures. It didn't look real. The airport bus driver had asked me for five hundred francs to ride into town from the airport. When I tried to argue, a fellow American passenger explained that the difference between new francs and old was a matter of chopped-off zeroes. New francs were brand new in France. The bus driver was still dealing in old francs. So his five hundred francs were my five. Mystified, I handed the driver a five-franc bill and he started the bus. I'd needed a ticket for the Métro ride. Not knowing that the word for Métro ticket was simply *ticket de Métro,* I performed a finger puppet routine to describe to the woman behind the glass what it was I needed. That transaction concluded, I then asked her for *Saint Michel?* She pointed to a map under glass nearby where I could press the button corresponding to the stop I wanted to go to. The best route from one station to another lit up to show me the way. A uniformed man seated at the entrance to the subway *quai* took my ticket, chopped a hole in it with his hole puncher and gave it back.

In 1961, the Paris *Métro* had red or green wooden cars that made a clackety sound as they rolled along the tracks. But when the train took off or stopped, it made a different sound — a clunk and a rattle. There were slatted wooden seats in second class, upholstered ones in first. Special seats in both classes were reserved for pregnant women, the blind, seniors and war veterans. Those categories of passenger could simply flash a card with a tricolor stripe on the diagonal across the top corner to someone already sitting in one of those seats, and that person was obliged to rise and let them sit there. Whenever that happened, I caught myself staring. It was surprising. Nobody huffed or puffed or questioned the practice. Later on, I took the *Métro* the way a child rides on a carousel. Over and over again.

I drank it all in. Every solitary second of this newness, every stammer I had to hurdle in order to be understood, every raised eyebrow, smirk, mustache, couple kissing in the street, noisy traffic jam, neatly uniformed policeman's puffed-out chest, acrid fume-choked breath of air and cluttered sidewalk café belonged to this, the first day of the rest of my life.

Next to me in the café, at circular marble-topped café tables, sat groups of laughing, smoking college students. They were all talking at once. Nobody appeared calm or reserved or discreet. They were all involved in what seemed to be lusty arguments, crackling disputes and rude exchanges. Their speech was agitated, edgy, nervous, yet joyful.

I couldn't understand the words. But I could feel the excitement they emitted. Back in Buffalo, New York, at my parents' house, this brand of excitement and frenzied squabbling was forbidden. Even take-your-breath-away giggling was frowned upon.

Perhaps it was then and there I decided to become French. I would learn to speak French without an accent, dress like a true *Parisienne* and be openly sexy and noisy whenever I felt like it.

I went back to the hotel list in the guidebook and decided to try for the least expensive room in the tilting, narrow *Hôtel de la Californie.* Yes. That's right. Hotel California. Shades of sounds to come.

Despite its dingy décor of cracked ocher plaster, missing eye-level moldings and plastic vases full of multicolored dusty vinyl flowers, the lobby bespoke a certain tired tidiness. An aged philodendron had crept about the walls and been tucked under and over crannies all around the lectern-type wooden desk behind which sat the gray-cardiganed, bespectacled proprietor. *"Mademoiselle?"* he peered at me to inquire.

I held up ten fingers, each meant to represent one franc, and said, "Une chambre, s'il vous plaît."

The old gentleman reached around behind him, picked a skeleton key attached to a heavy metal star from off its number 16 hook, handed it to me and said, "Troisième," which meant third floor.

It took me a few minutes' hunting fruitlessly about the third floor's linoleum corridor to remember that in France, first floors are called ground floors, and hence third floors were really fourth floors. I mounted the extra staircase, thumping heavy bags behind me, and located number 16 at the rear of the narrow hallway.

Inside the tiny two-dollar hotel room, a lumpy double bed was spread with a skirted, dark red faille coverlet. In one corner a plywood partition, painted a tired yellow, was curtained off by a worn but garish flowered cotton print. The partition leaned precariously against a once-beige wall. Behind this fabric screen lived a bathroom sink and a squat plumbing device I knew to be a sort of fanny-washing bathtub called a *bidet.* I closed the faded curtain and smiled.

France was all different. Paris made noise, but not familiar noise; the sounds were somehow not my sounds. French people smiled, but they didn't smile those wide American grins I knew so well. Buildings were not old. They were ancient. Rooms were scuffed and marred, paint was cracked, stair carpets worn through, beds and cupboards and lamps sloped and tilted higgledy-piggledy like the buildings on the tree-lined sloping streets.

Paris was ancient. But it was not dirty. Papers did not blow helter-skelter in gutters. Whirlpools of soot did not rise from the pavements as they did in New York. All the ancientness around me had been scrubbed. I checked the corners of my room. No balls of other people's dust. Lifting the coverlet, I fingered the bed sheets. The thick, rough muslin, despite frayed edges and numerous spots of someone's patient darning, had been laundered blue-white. My father would have hated France's hodgepodge. My friends would have scoffed. They would have found France tacky and out-of-date. My mother would have called France shabby. I wanted to call it home.

Ironically, it was my father who had saved the day. He'd refused to lend me money for this trip. But he wanted to be sure I had a job waiting for me in Paris. He had a friend among his new Midwestern colleagues who had worked in France and spoke some French. My dad's crony composed a phony letter of glowing recommendation for me. He then sent the letter to one of his former business acquaintances in Paris, Monsieur Giovanni Traub. Though I neither typed, took shorthand nor spoke French, Giovanni Traub had agreed, across thousands of miles of ocean, to hire a twenty-two-year-old American girl who, the reference letter had assured him, was a professional bilingual secretary.

Monsieur Traub's reasons for hiring me were both logical and self-seeking. He was an illegally self-employed, non-certified consulting engineer with a few different passports. Whenever the subject was broached by any French authority, Monsieur Traub's national origins swapped around from Switzerland to Italy to Germany and back to Switzerland again. His business in Paris was unclearly defined as *Specialiste en bâtiment* or building specialist. My two-hundred-dollar monthly wage was to be paid in untaxable, untraceable, unmentionable cash under the table.

The two-room office where I worked was a small part of an ancient, sprawling apartment in a nineteenth century townhouse in Paris's lavish residential 8th arrondissement. There was no sign on the door and the company's letterheads changed according to Monsieur Traub's needs — almost weekly.

Many years before his arrival in Paris, an unidentified scourge had invaded Giovanni Traub's person, causing layers of his skin to flake off. This malady made him look atrocious and inspired frequent fits of self-pity. Aside from the peculiar skin ailment, Traub was short, fat, Swiss of movement, Italian of temper, French of imagined sensuality and thickly German of accent. I never asked to see my boss's ID.

When he first met me, Monsieur Traub informed me, "I ham spikking turteen lanquishes!"

I was impressed. I asked him in which of his thirteen languages he was most fluent. Traub, pushing out his burly chest, had replied, "Heenglush da best!"

At this time, his "Heenglush" was so much superior to my own skeletal French that I could not have guessed whether Traub's real mother tongue was Basque or Etruscan. In fact, my ability to communicate in French was still limited to that of a precocious one-year-old. Stuttered equivalents of "bye-bye, dada, caca, peepee, apple and birdie" about summed it up.

Since most people who telephoned the Paris office were eager to convey a message, whenever I answered the phone I immediately stammered out, *"Parlez-vous anglais?"* Unfortunately, most callers did not speak Heenglish "da best" or even "da worst." So, unless Monsieur Traub was in the office to take the call in French, I hung up. And, since my typing skills tipped the scales at about ten inaccuracies per minute, Traub wrote most of his business letters in longhand. I kept myself busy all day brushing fallen scraps of Monsieur Traub's skin off desktops and dreaming of a dashing Frog Prince who would take me off my own hands.

In light of our unorthodox labor-sharing practices, I felt neither underpaid nor overworked. Traub, though hideously unattractive, was kind to me. He found me a room in a family-flavored boarding house on the Left Bank where I had hoped to meet some swanky new people. However, my fellow boarders consisted of: Lisa, an American woman in Paris recovering from a lifelong case of nerves; Bernadette, a lapsed Carmelite nun who had never kicked the silence habit; a minuscule, handsome Vietnamese judo instructor and six or eight swarthy foreign worker types who tackled tough steaks, baguettes and strong cheeses with thick greasy fingers and drank liter upon liter of sturdy red wine.

Of all these potential companions, only the young judo instructor, Lung Ho, manifested an interest in befriending me. I knew nobody. Lung Ho was better than nobody. His crude advances under the communal breakfast table and the ceremonious sacrifice of his daily butter ration onto my plate forewarned that he was out to make my acquaintance.

He kept leaving notes on my door. Mr. Traub translated the first of these from Lung's approximate French into his own testy English. "The pearls of your woman smell bean sprouts in ancient fish brine." Flattery? Lung's inscrutability put me on guard. His second message said, "Three serpent moons offer weeping willows ancestor legacy." At least that was Monsieur Traub's translation. My curiosity was gaining on my skepticism.

A third note was artistically calligraphed, "A wise grandmother sows grains by crippled handfuls." My resistance was diminishing. Lung Ho was exotic. I was in Paris where exotic meant interesting. At dinner one evening I slid my butter curl across the table to Lung's place. Lung Ho answered my gesture of woo the next morning. I found three fresh trout and a further paper hieroglyph attached to my door. I filled up the bidet, stuck the fish in the water and took the note to the office with me. Monsieur Traub concluded, with the aid of a couple of obscure dictionaries, that "Consuming birds tether the evening star's gaze before lunar light" meant that Lung Ho wanted me to accept his invitation for dinner at about eight.

"Should I go out with him tonight?" I asked.

"Neffer!" Traub said. He crumpled Lung's note into a crystal ashtray, lit it with his Dunhill and watched it burn, saying, "Fietnammer peoples iss Vhite Slafers!"

"What's a white slaver?" I wondered.

"Yellowish persons vhat takes Amerikanische cutie-pie girls like you to Hanoi for torture dem in bamboo caytches."

It was the bit about the bamboo cages that persuaded me not to accept Lung Ho's invitation. Nonetheless, he showed up at my door that evening, took my left hand and turned the palm upward. In the dim light he read my fate: *Vous très jeune. Vous très jolie. Vous souffrir beaucoup monsieur. Beaucoup lune. Pas assez soleil.* In short, Lung Ho thought I was a sad case. Returning my hand without yanking out so much as one fingernail, Lung patted my head in a universal gesture of kindness and left me to my own devices saying "Pretty young girl" in broken French. "Suffer with men. Too much moon. No shining sun."

CHAPTER ELEVEN

P ARIS — SIX-MONTH INVENTORY. I printed my list of sexploits in the expensive leather notebook I had bought out of Monsieur Traub's petty cash.

(1) September — Ahmed — Rug seller — met at Clignancourt Métro station — (Cute but married. One time. Pumper. No cum 4 me)

(2) October — Dr. Serge Blindee — Gyn. — pub. health clinic — (big talk, little do, free penicillin shots, cums 2 quick, no cum 4 me)

(3) All Saints Day — Jerry Frye — American journalist pick-up Brasserie Lipp, St. Germain des Près — (Intellectual, cleanish, married. Floppy balls, OK dick, Passing thru, expense account dinner, takes 2 long 2 cum, no cum 4 me)

(4) November — Alphonse Rapace — mailman — 8th arrondissement — (*rustique,* gives free stamps, huge one thick, short — potbelly, no deodorant, quick sex in office corridor — no cum 4 me)

(5) Advent — Tony Saunders — Australian painter — embassy party — (6 ft. 6" w. matching cock, pigsty house, smelly feet, etc., in/out for hrs., flies on ceiling, cystitis 4 days, no cum 4 me)

(6) Noël — Guy Lepeloteur — Eng. lit. stud. Sorbonne — Café Bonaparte — (gay, likes 2 neck girls 'qui parlent anglais,' rich family, no see oui-oui, slurpy kisser, no cum 4 me)

(7) New Year's — Xavier Faure de la Taille — law student — Met in summer thru Jacques from *La Sorbonne* (dishy blond, my age, wrs. gloves, lives. w. parents, noble family, no money, teaches me French 4 free, No sex … yet)

I had made it through almost six months of Paris life. Here it was the Feast of the Ascension and I was still without a full-time French lover. The bubbly mirror in my room kept an eye on progress. I was, it reflected, a perky young woman. But the blackbird of dissatisfaction had been hippity-hopping on the edges of my mouth for too long and a French crow must have been treading the corners of my eyes while I slept.

I was sitting at my office desk when the phone jolted me. *"Allo,"* I said. *"Oui, c'est le bureau de Monsieur Traub. Non, Monsieur Traub n'est pas là. Au revoir, monsieur."*

Thanks to the kind tutelage of my new friend Xavier, my knowledge of French was increasing.

More rings.

"Allo ... Oui, c'est moi-même. Bonjour, ça va? Sept heures et demie. Ici? D'accord." Receiving a message in French and understanding it was like a miracle to me. Each time someone rang or I phoned someone and they made a date and then they actually appeared like magic at the designated place on time, I had goosebumps. I couldn't believe that my stringing together a series of new-fangled odd sounds could actually make things happen. Bit by bit, speaking French was no longer just a fatiguing gymnastic. The mellifluous French language was becoming a means of communication.

The previous was from Xavier. He would meet me after work. We would go to a café and share a glass of hot wine. The drinks were always on me. But Xavier's Gallic splendor was well worth the price of admission. Albeit his motive in our friendship was persistently indeterminate, I didn't mind. Xavier Faure de la Taille was the handsomest man I had ever seen.

Not only was he a tower of a young man, but Xavier sported a shock of thick blond hair that fell fetchingly across his forehead. He wore a double-breasted navy blue blazer, gray flannel pants, black dress shoes and gloves! Yes. Gloves. Pigskin gloves. In Paris. In summer and in winter. Xavier's gloves were the short kind, the kind that Charles Boyer whipped off to shake someone's hand in old movies.

I had never imagined such an elegant young person existed in real life. I may have seen a pre-WWII movie about swanky people who lived in *châteaux*, said "Pardon my glove" when shaking hands and "dressed for dinner." I had read English novels about Oxonians who spent weeks at people's stately country houses. But for real? Somebody *I* knew. Someone who enjoyed my company and kept coming back for more? Only in fairy tales.

Monsieur Traub detested Xavier. I was Traub's own personal shoulder to cry on. A captive audience who lent a sympathetic ear to his eternal woes. Until I had met the noble Xavier, I had lavished my full attention during office hours on the gory details of my employer's dermatological neurasthenia. After his hard day's three-hour lunch, Traub was always a wreck. So he sat at his desk and called for me to come take a letter. I came and sat and he cried.

Today, just as I readied myself to sneak off the premises at seven-thirty p.m., Giovanni Traub amplified his sobs and made it impossible for me to abandon him in good conscience. "Ooohhhh! Mein Gott, how I'm suffer," was his opening supplication.

"Is there anything I can do for you before I leave, *Monsieur*?" I called brightly from the outer office.

"Come ... come to me here for seeing me quick," he said.

I, in full winter outer dress, peeked around the door. "I can see you from here," I said.

"Come closer, Mein Küchen. On a man you are looking who iss finished but before he beginss. A done fish is seating at dis desk. A apple vhat iss falling from life's tree."

I approached warily. "Now, now. *Monsieur* Traub, you're a grown man. If I've told you once, I've told you a hundred times to dry your tears and go home to your family. You're tired. You need to get some sleep."

"Sleep? Sleep? She says sleep to a man vhat has da ... how you call ...?"

"Corrosive epidermolysis," I assisted.

"A corroded man mit a colt Heenglush voman for vife and shildrens too corroding. You tink I vas sleeping maybe much? By da night I don't sleep. Not on your bottom I don't." Traub blew his nose and lowered his head onto folded arms atop the desk.

At seven-forty, I was still sitting there in front of him. "*Monsieur* Traub, if you will excuse my saying so, I think you're a bit old to be carrying on like this."

Traub was pushing forty. But when you're twenty-two, everybody else is old. He looked up. "So perhaps you tink I can stop from falling off mein skins? Iss funny for you verking all day hard brooming from da papers crumbs of your boss? I'm screaming in your face I haf dissease making messes in all over Paris restaurants. Men I eat for lunch dey haf mistress. Me? I haf no mistress. Neffer my life." Traub's tear ducts, at least, were in perfect working order. The heave of his Italian-cut snowflaked shoulders tore at my pity center.

"But you have a lovely wife who cares for you. A good job. Two growing boys. If you ask me, I think you should count your blessings."

Raising his head from the desk, Traub rallied. "So American you are, Soossie Hosskinss. Like pilgrum boy scout. For vat you tink I haf da Heenglish vife? She staying home for shildrens making da foods. Me? I am man. Man is needing go out by da night. Man is needing da luf. For me is no luf. Always girls dey are seeing one small flakes, dey running gaway. You not help me. I hask you find for me some friends of you for making da luf. Fat vones even vhat are laughing. I gif for dat money. Dollars. Sviss francs, trafeler's checks ... I haf much money but I haf no luf."

"*Monsieur* Traub, I know you'll understand, I really have to run. There is a friend waiting downstairs and it's very cold out."

"Friend of you? She is maybe pretty?" Traub swept his shoulders with a gold-handled, natural-bristle whiskbroom from Dior.

"It's my friend, Xavier. You know him — the tall blond boy who is helping me with my French. I mustn't keep him waiting." I rose to leave.

"Ooohhh, mein gott in himmel, vat a life I haf ven nobody gifs me damn. Such a baby boy you vould go out mit vhen you can from me enchoy one *Tour d'Argent* dinner mit duck unt oranges. Your baby boy he can't give you dat," Traub said.

The doorbell rang. I invited Xavier into the entryway and semaphored he should be quiet. Too polite not to say goodnight, on my way out, I pushed *Monsieur* Traub's door open a crack. "We'll be leaving now, sir. See you in the morning."

Traub, going over some papers now with an air of studied calm, remarked, "I tought you already hours ago left. Vhy alvays are you staying so late here? Go enchoy out. Alvays verking, verking. Tsk. Tsk." He resumed his paperwork.

So far I had not found one smatter of romance in my appointments with Xavier. Xavier reserved physical contact to the removal of my coat in cafés and occasional paternal pats on my head. Six months younger than me, Xavier seemed to have been born at the age of fifty. The grammar notebook had been his idea. I was supposed to have been charting French verb conjugations in its pages.

"Have you done your homework?" Xavier asked me in his elegant French.

"I didn't have time. But I did buy the notebook," I said in broken French. I smiled at the waiter when he brought our hot wine. "*Merci, monsieur*," I thanked him.

As soon as the *garçon* was out of hearing range, Xavier spoke up. "In France, you never call a waiter *monsieur*. He is not your equal."

I answered, "My brother-in-law Tony was a waiter. He's my sister's husband. He's sort of my equal, *non*?" I took my turn and sipped at the wine, watching Xavier through the steam.

"In France, you must never tell. A waiter in your family is not dignified." He jotted that down for me in the notebook.

"Well, Tony's not exactly a waiter anymore. He has four pizza joints. But he used to be a waiter at a spaghetti house in my hometown. He's really rich now. We're very proud of him. He's got a big Caddy and my sister has an English sports car. They do all right. They're in Bermuda now. I got a postcard this morning."

Xavier had a bit more English than I had French. But only a smidge. When he didn't understand something, he delivered an aristocratic sniff. "In France we call such people *commerçants*. Their money is too fresh over the counter. Shopkeepers, restaurateurs — we don't mix with them."

"What about butchers?" I asked. "My father is a butcher. Of course he isn't anymore because of the supermarkets. But he used to own three butcher shops. Pretty good, huh?"

"But now you say he is no longer a butcher?" Xavier looked hopeful.

"Nope. He's a kind of magazine dealer. You know, door-to-door, I'm working my way through college. He can get you almost any magazine for free."

"You mean he is in publishing then? An editor perhaps." Hope flashed anew in Xavier's big brown eyes.

"No. Not publishing. He has employees who sell magazines. I guess you would call him a sales manager."

After a brief, decorous coughing fit, Xavier gradually recovered his composure. "You will never ever tell anyone here that your father is a salesman. In France, that is not done."

"Nobody sells things in France?"

It took Xavier approximately one hour to explain that, *en France* it was considered lowly to work. Acceptable perhaps were careers for doctors, ship's captains, notaries, lawyers, antique dealers and priests. Women? Did women work? Well, he told me, women only worked if their husbands had been killed in the war. And in those few cases it was proper only if the women did a bit of decorating for friends, or acted as assistants in a high-fashion house. Occasionally, because of the unfortunate circumstance of being a sole female heir without brothers, a widow might even run her family-owned art gallery. Xavier, for example, was a student of the law. He would not, however, seek to become a lawyer. Rather, he would pursue his career as a student until the age of thirty. Then he would retire and live on a small income from his Aunt Marguerite's fortune.

"Why wait till you're thirty?" I was curious to know.

"Because Aunt Marguerite is not yet dead. I go to her house every Sunday for lunch. She is a lonely old woman. To please her, I study the law. In my family the youngest son always studies the law." Xavier opened the top button of his double-breasted blazer, leaned back and puffed on his Gitane cigarette.

"What if she doesn't die in time?"

"She will," Xavier assured me. "She will. Now, about the past definite tense of the verb *valoir*."

Six months of singularly uneventful, asexual *politesses* had passed between Xavier Faure de la Taille and *moi*. I saw him often. For French lessons.

It was midwinter before I could finally afford to move from my boarding house room to a small studio in an ancient, decrepit building located in *la rue du Clos Feuquières,* a cobbled dead-end street in Paris's 15th arrondissement. My new quarters were not much on style, bathing facilities or heat. The narrow one-windowed ground floor room fronted on the street.

The place was gloomy and lonely. But it was mine. Besides, I planned to redecorate. I would paint the walls my favorite minty green, spruce up the foldout couch's faded cover, construct a pink, paper lantern shade for the light bulb, re-varnish and repair the listing table and chairs. I assured myself it wouldn't be so bad once I had spent a bit of cash and invested some elbow grease.

The move to my own place called for a housewarming celebration. Aside from Xavier and *Monsieur* Traub, I had no Parisian friends. As the two men were rivals for my attention, I decided to invite just one of them to share my first home-cooked meal in Paris. I, of course, chose Xavier over Traub.

Although my French had improved, I was still often caught off guard by French customs, speech and measures. I hurried into the butcher shop around the corner from my new digs. *"Poulet, s'il vous plaît."* I ordered chicken.

"Combien?" asked the butcher. How much chicken did I want?

"Je ne say pas," I stammered. I knew nothing of kilos or grams. I hesitated and smiled at the butcher who emitted an impatient sigh. I explained, *"Je ne suis pas française."* — "I'm not French."

"I know," he snarled. "I have two ears!" After that retort, he inquired *"Poulet pour combien?"* He held up some fingers to ask how many I would be feeding with his chicken.

Relieved, I held up two fingers and found myself paying for a very small, less-than-two-pound chicken for two.

I was learning. Parisians were like that. Either you spoke their language perfectly and walked their precarious lifeline between tradition and charm, or else they treated you like *merde,* which means shit. How could gracious Paris abide mingling with so many obstreperous Parisians? They both frightened and fascinated me. But never mind. I was drunk on their magnificent city. Everywhere I turned, I encountered loveliness and *luxe.*

No matter how lonely I felt, I could take a safe evening stroll along the quays of the *Seine* and watch the golden boats full of tourists floating through shimmering waters. Past the lighted Eiffel Tower, under the glorious gold-leafed bridge of *Alexandre III* and onward toward the illuminated *Notre Dame de Paris.* In Paris, walking distances were short, the buildings tilted low against the cloudy skies. Paris, I decided again and again, had been built to be lived in by people like me.

Xavier was late arriving on the evening of my celebration dinner. From Neuilly, the posh area where he lived with his parents, he had to cross the whole of Paris to get to my working class neighborhood. Still, by subway, this trip ought not to have taken more than half an hour. As I let him in, I queried, "Did you have trouble finding it?"

Xavier removed his great uncle's hand-me-down overcoat and replied, "*Non.* But the buses are slow at this hour. Traffic is dense around the *Etoile.* Cars are bumper to bumper up and down the *Champs Elysées.*"

I motioned to him to sit down on one of my two chairs. "The bus?" I wondered from my perch across from him on the lumpy bed. "Why do you take the bus? It's ever so much longer that way."

"We never take the *Métro.* The *Métro* is for common people. It stinks!" He pinched his nose to illustrate.

"But the *Métro* is quicker than the bus in rush hour." I headed to the kitchen cubicle. "What will you have to drink?" I asked him.

"*Un whiskey Perrier, s'il vous plaît.*"

In France all whiskey is Scotch whiskey. I prepared him a short one with fizzy water. Handing the small mustard glass to Xavier, I sat down again, pulled my skirt demurely over my knees, waved an arm around and asked, "Well? How do you like my new place?"

From behind an elegant sip of his drink, Xavier's eyebrows rose to hide an impending scoff. "It's very small," he gulped.

"We have a word for it in English. We say cozy. It means intimate and warm."

"The French have no word for that," he said, "We say either "warm" or else simply "intimate." French is a very specific language. We like to say what we mean."

Xavier was so debonair and handsome it didn't matter if he boasted. True, he was more snobbish than I cared to admit. Worse, he had not so much as insinuated he might like to take me to bed. To ensure that no further discussion of testy matters might arouse his Latin temperament, I changed the subject and told him that the butcher had said, "I have two ears," to point up my American accent.

I got up to check on the chicken, simmering on the two-burner hot plate, and said, "Don't you think that was rude?"

"You are too sensitive, Suzanne," said Xavier smiling. "The butcher was only teasing you about how you sound. Perhaps it was you who behaved rudely by not knowing how much chicken you needed for your *cuisine.*"

To express those last thoughts, Xavier had employed the past tenses of some particularly tricky reflexive verbs with which I had been having a lot of trouble. Just as well that I didn't understand it all. He was scolding *me.*

During dinner, we maintained a truce of jocularity. Thanks to a good bottle of Bordeaux and a not too badly flavored sauce, my guest's pontificating about French traditions and manners had been kept in check. Over coffee and cognac, I giggled as I attempted to ape Xavier's high-class accent in the rendering of a tongue twister he had insisted I learn by heart. My efforts were comical. Even stuffy Xavier found reason to chuckle as I tripped over "*Les chaussettes de l'archiduchesse sont sèches et archi sèches,*" for the tenth time.

In the high spirits of this jovial *tête-a-tête*, Xavier dropped his inherited guard of standoffishness long enough for me to dare asking, "Are you having a good time?"

As though I had smote him on the side of his well-shapen skull with a frying pan, Xavier started, "Whatever do you mean by that?" He crossed his leg at the knee and shook his well-worn black shoe in a kind of ride-a-cock-horse rhythm.

Had I succeeded once again in offending him? I corrected my phrasing. "Is this evening any fun for you?" Leaning back in the creaky wooden chair, Xavier pulled his blue packet of cigarettes from the pocket of his brother's hand-me-down, elbow-patched, Harris tweed jacket, lowered his blond eyelashes over piercing ebony eyes, tossed back his thick, blond forelock and deigned to suppose that this soirée was *assez amusante*. Amusing enough.

I let this bland comment pass as though it had been uttered in Serbo-Croat and got up to clear the table. As I passed my arm in front of Xavier to scoop up an empty plate, my stuffy guest surprised me by nervously thrusting his hand behind my back and patting me soundly on the ass.

I dropped the plate. What the hell was the proper thing to do now? Did I melt away in a heap of mid-Victorian vapors? Was it incumbent upon me, according to the manners of Xavier's country, to lash him across the face with the paper napkin I held crumpled in my hand? Did French women blush and wriggle in such compromising circumstances? Or did they pull a Brigitte Bardot, rip off their laced-up camisoles and lunge at the throats of their conquerors?

I didn't know what I was supposed to do, but what I did do was decidedly American and blatantly bold. I dropped the paper napkin, placed my woollen-skirted knee into the depths of Xavier's lap, enlaced his neck with both hands and said, in English, "Would you like to make love to me?"

Xavier, despite his semi-ignorance of English, clasped my buttocks firmly with both hands and rubbed them expertly up and down.

Swooning slightly to add a romantic note, I hugged his face to my flat chest and suggested, "Let's go to bed," in my most carefully articulated French.

Unfortunately, my promising passionate French prince turned out to be a pathetically nervous neophyte lover. Xavier's sole previous sexual experience had occurred when he had accidentally sat down in a cheap café in *la rue des Écoles*. He needed a warm drink. He got a hot hooker. He described the experience as any proud young man might. "She told me I am a very good lover."

In our own first attempt at lovemaking that evening, Xavier hastily crushed me under him and captured my body between his bony knees. By the time he felt around to find his hardened prick in the scratchy folds of his gray flannel school trousers, it was much too late. Xavier had come all over himself and me. He even got some on his older brother's hand-me-down red silk tie.

Notwithstanding, I did not terminate my budding relationship with my knight in hand-me-down armor. In spite of his poor first performance in bed, I was still intrigued and excited by Xavier's dash and flair, his impeccable conduct and his oddly touching innocence about my world. Thus, for whatever it was worth, we two young people, little by little, found ourselves clinging together most nights in hot pursuit of some measure of intimate *détente.*

Xavier loved me. He told me so many, many times a day. I loved him too. Underneath the bluff façade, he had a sweet soul. He was romantic. He called me his *petit chat* and wrote me love notes that he slid into my purse or sometimes even sent me by post. I felt that if I could extricate Xavier from his stuffy family who deemed they knew how everything *ought* to be done by everybody, there was perhaps a chance that he would loosen up and learn to make love like every self-respecting Frenchman should. One day I might even take Xavier to America and turn him into a solid, middle-income language teacher in a proper private school.

CHAPTER TWELVE

T raub jumped ship. He claimed he was going back to Rome where he would maybe find some luf.

Of course, if I wanted it, I still had my job. But the company for which Traub had been working off the books had sent in his replacement — a handsome, middle-aged, goose-stepping Nazi named Josef Zucker. I hated Josef Zucker. And it was reciprocal. This morning I was going to the office to quit my job.

So far, life in Paris had been good to me. But I blew it. I told my father about the changes at work. He sent me the money to come home. I was sad. Frustrated. Defeated. Pissed off at the world.

A week later, while waiting for Xavier to join me on the sunny café terrace of *Chez Francis* at the *Place de L'Alma,* I re-read my father's letter. "Here's the money for your ticket home," it said. Before signing off, he had added a note. "P.S. Don't say I didn't warn you about foreigners, Susie."

Maybe my dad was right, I thought. I had taken a big risk dashing off alone to work in Paris for an unknown foreign madman whose skin flaked off. But I had learned so much. I really thought it was worth it. I couldn't stay on in Paris. I had no job. But I didn't want to go back. And I certainly did not want to leave my handsome prince behind.

Xavier tried to dissuade me. "You will find another job," he assured me. "Your French is nearly perfect now. Stay. Give it one more month. Please don't leave me like this."

"I am sorry, *mon chéri,*" I said. "But I must go home. My father is upset. He says my mother is lonely. My family misses me. I must go back to Wisconsin."

My heart gave a thump. *Back to Wisconsin?* I had never even set foot in Wisconsin. But the parents had moved there from Chicago; I felt obliged. My dad had sounded glum on the crackly transatlantic phone call I made from the local Paris Post Office. No more free office phone. No more sobbing Monsieur Traub. No more Xavier. No more magnificent Paris. I gave up my tawdry little home. Took a taxi to Orly airport and got on a plane. I sobbed all the way back to the land of the round doorknobs. I had no idea what was in store.

I found myself back at home, living with my family just outside Milwaukee, in Elm Grove, Wisconsin, where everybody believed in the money god. Upon first glimpse of the posh suburb, I imagined there might be a preoccupation with income brackets and the like. But the members of this restricted — no Jews, Blacks, etc. — community were beyond such banalities. "A great place to raise kids," mused the Lion at my homecoming dinner. "Clean-living people, these Midwesterners."

"Elm Grove sure is tidy, Dad," I said, as we sat down to share my welcome home dinner of Elva's tasty, well-done prime rib and luscious brown gravy with mashed potatoes. My mother was a good cook. Nothing fancy. The Lion did not allow fancy food in the house. No chili. No quiches. And — God forbid — no spaghetti.

"These potatoes make me gag," griped twelve-year-old John.

"Why don't we ever have any garlic potato chips around this house anymore?" chimed in Peter, who, at sixteen, had become irascible, difficult, less- than-pleasant company.

Elva stood tableside, attending her brood. After so many years of family service, her smile had begun to freeze. She was resigned to living under the rule of male verdicts. Her eyes straight ahead, the Lamb apologized. "I am sorry, Peter. It's my fault. By the time I got to the store on Friday, they were out of garlic chips. They only had regular, ruffled, chive and barbecue." Peter harrumphed.

"Tomorrow I'll drive into the city and stock up," Elva said, as she sat down. Forks clinked away. The Lion dug into a second mountain of mashed and covered it with rich brown gravy. "Don't you like driving your new car, Babe?" he asked his wife through a mouthful. "You don't go shopping much lately."

"I like the Buick fine, thank you, dear." The Lamb stood and began clearing plates.

The Lion snarled. "Will you sit down? I haven't finished my dinner."

"I was just going out to whip the cream," the Lamb explained. Obediently, she began to redistribute the pile of plates, each to its former owner.

"Elva!" said Big George, "aren't those plates you're setting back down all greasy on the bottom? You stacked them together, Babe. Don't put them back on the tablecloth." The Lion shook his head.

"You really must be more careful, Babe. Just sit down now. Relax. Susie can get the dessert." He addressed me directly, "Can't you, Honey?"

The Lamb just stood there and slowly reconstructed her greasy pile of Limoges china plates into a second neat stack. Then she sat, staring ahead. I had started to rise when I noticed a missile heading directly for my chops. I ducked. The object missed my head by centimeters. I looked up and saw that my mom was busy hurling her most elegant dinner plates one by one against the woodsy mural behind my head.

In between throws, the Lamb bleated loudly, "Honey this!" Crash. "Honey that!" Thud/tinkle. "You always call Susie Honey!" Crash. "Me? I'm just old Babe. Just a mangy old pet you call Babe. And now that Susie's home, you favor her and take her out with you for ice cream and drive her down to Chicago to hear Dixieland. You never take *me* to go hear Dixieland."

"But Babe," said my father, "you hate Dixieland. You say it hurts your ears."

"You always loved her more!" Elva raised her pitching arm, let fly a crystal goblet full of ice water and mimicked her husband's voice.

"My daughter Susan goes to Buffalo Seminary. My daughter Susie lives in Paris. My daughter Susie speaks French. My daughter Susan is a teacher!"

Shrill and cutting, Elva blathered on. "And what am I? What do I do? I peel and cook pound after pound of potatoes and you never even come home on time to eat them. *'Ask your father, Peter. I really can't tell you, boys. That's your father's department. We'll have to talk it over with Dad.'* Me? Who am I? I'm just the dimwit scullery maid. I don't get to make decisions. I can't have the kind of potato chips *I* like. We live in this upper crust, Kraut concentration camping ground because *you* chose it. We read the newspapers *you* approve of. We drive Buicks because they're *your* favorites and we should be thankful that *you* provide them." Tears of embarrassment and rage spilled over on her print apron front.

My mother was beautiful. Heaps of wavy raven hair. Big brown Irish eyes. Anger suited her. I felt sick. I avoided looking up at her by drawing circles on the table linen with my knife. But as I had studied psychology and had learned that rage was sanity, I murmured, "It's all right, Mommy. Say what's on your mind."

My mom's outburst was breaking my heart. I felt so sorry for her.

Stuck out here in a white-bread suburb with three needy men who expected her to do all the work and didn't help out. I had never before seen Elva Hoskins outwardly angry nor heard her raise her voice. She was weeping openly now. Looking straight at me, tears running wild everywhere on her pretty face, she said, "Susie, I want you to go away."

"But I came home to see you, Mom." I felt little. And lonely. I gnawed at a fingernail.

"Don't give me that!" Elva suddenly shrewed at me. "You came here to see your father!" Railing from out of some deeply buried ancient rite of mother-daughter spite and fear of growing old, Elva spat her words at me, "Do you want your father? Well, take him! You get out and take him with you — back to Paris. Introduce him to all your nightclub cafe-society friends. And while you're at it, you can sleep with him too! That's what you've always wanted. Take him. He's yours!" Yanking the tablecloth out from under the remains of dinner, Elva Hoskins, former lamb and obedient scullery maid, retired to her *boudoir*.

I gaped at my father. "Daddy," I whispered, "is Mommy ... I mean, has she gone ...?"

"She's overtired. Pay no attention. Peter, get the broom. John, pick up the salad. Susie, start the dishes." The Lion growled out these orders and, heaving a sigh, maintained ashen self-control and left the room.

Stunned, we kids silently pitched in to right the shambles. Scooping up scraps, I vaguely heard the Lion's timid knocks on his own bedroom door. Somehow, I hoped, he could straighten things out. As I raked gravy from the rug with clawed fingers, the image of my raging mother haunted me. Elva was not the same youthful woman who had left me behind in Buffalo a few years before. Her middle-aged smiles were taut and too carefully planned. There was distance in her sweet eyes, a Wendy look of having left the pirates and the boys behind with Peter Pan.

"Did you get the gravy off the wall?" Peter asked, slashing a hole in the strained stillness.

I looked up at my brother. All tall and muscled now, sixteen-year-old Peter was a total stranger to me. I'd been away. First college. Then Paris. Too much time had passed. I didn't know these people anymore. Sweeping some smaller shards of glass onto a dustpan held for me by young John, I answered Peter's question with one of my own, "Do you think we should call a doctor?"

"Dad knows best," came Peter's reply. "That's his department. I only work here," he snickered. "We are not paid to ask questions." He gestured a subtle wave toward the kitchen.

I looked around. Elva was back. She was got up in her husband's best pinstripe suit. She had his leather golf bag slung over one shoulder. Cleanup operations were suspended as we children watched our mother's encore performance. The Lion stood by, helpless, as my mother told him off. "I have all of your love letters in here," she said. Reaching into the golf bag, she went about placing the best years of her life, page by page, into the dishwasher's tidy racks. This done, she slammed the machine's door, gave the dial a brisk twist to full cycle, and brushed airily past her hand-wringing husband singing "I'm gonna wash that man right outta my hair" in a tense falsetto.

The Lion walked into the living room, flipped on the TV and sat soundlessly down to bury his hatchet in the latest episode of *Lawman*. I dashed to rescue the dishwasher from shredded paper stoppage, wishing, whilst drying off every flap and fold of baby-blue stationery, that I had stayed in Paris. It felt as though my coming home had served only to increase the gap between the Hoskins clan and myself. Who were these people? What was I to them? How long would I have to stay here before finding out? And was it even necessary to bother?

George Junior, now a full partner in his father's door-to-door magazine business, lived nearby in a not-so-chic neighborhood with his family of six well-mannered children. His wife, the beautiful dark-skinned Thelma Martinelli Hoskins, had given birth to their six successive step-stair children rapid-fire, never more than a year apart. Shortly after her last confinement, Thelma had swallowed the family dog's entire vial of tranquilizers. She didn't die. But as soon as she recovered, Thelma took off for nobody knew where. Through it all, Georgie, the Rooster, had maintained his naughty grin, a few faded acne scars and a not-unbecoming mass of curly brown hair inherited from the Lamb's side. He twinkled engagingly as he spoke. "You can stay with us for a while, Susie. This thing is bound to blow over.

Mom never stays sick long. It's just a trick. It's her way of getting Dad's attention away from me."

George's paneled living room was Naugahyde childproof. A portrait of Jesus, looking suspiciously like Farley Granger with a beard, hung over the formica-topped dining table. I dreaded having to stay over there. "Maybe I ought to go to New Jersey and visit Sally and Tony for a couple of weeks," I suggested.

The Rooster poured me a second hefty Scotch. "You can't do that," he said.

"Why not? I have enough money to take the Greyhound bus," I retorted.

"Sally's sick," said Georgie.

"Another baby?" I asked. My sister had two kids. I had always expected she would have more.

"Shock treatment," said the Rooster and poured himself another drink.

I gasped. "Did she have a nervous breakdown?"

"No. She was overtired. Just like Thelma. Just like Mom," he answered.

I thought about my sister Sally then. She lived with her tall, handsome Dean Martin of a husband in suburban New Jersey. He worked in Manhattan. She stayed at home, isolated with two small children. She had gotten depressed. Now she, too, was going crazy.

My sojourn in the Father- and Motherland had so far been disastrous, but without sufficient funds, there was no escaping back to Paris. In hopes that the Lamb would emerge from the depression into which she had plummeted the day I arrived, I stayed with my brother George and his six kids for ten days.

During those days most of my time was spent cleaning and cooking for my cute, motherless nieces and nephews. The rest of the time had passed in heated late-night discussions with my elder brother as to why I always took my mother's side against my father.

"Women," George expounded, "go downhill as soon as you marry them. They get fat and grouchy and selfish. They don't have enough to do, so they start messing around with their husbands' heads." According to George, the Rooster, my mother was secretly trying to drive the Lion crazy or else make him have a heart attack so she could collect the insurance. "All Dad ever does is work a little late. He doesn't even cheat on her. I don't think he ever cheated on her in his life. And now that bitch is convinced he's out running around when he's really at work with me."

In the end, my mother phoned to ask me back. "I'm sorry. I've been sick," she said in a shaky voice. "You can come home now."

CHAPTER THIRTEEN

I did go home. Elva had been sedated. Quieter. We co-habited in relative peace. We even had one or two heart-to-hearts with our coffee in the mornings after the men had left for their various occupations in the real world.

"When we moved here, I looked into taking classes at the university," said Mom. "I wanted to do psychology. Maybe just go nights at first. Or part time during the day."

"Mom!" I said. "What a brilliant idea. I remember. You graduated high school at fifteen. But you had to go to work so you missed out on college. Now's your chance. Do it. Go back to school. Get a degree. You're so damn smart, you'll go straight to the head of the class."

"I applied," said Elva. "And I got accepted." She beamed. "I even bought the books. But when I told Daddy he said college is expensive and anyway it isn't for women. It wasn't really that expensive, Susie," she said. "If he could buy Peter a car and send you a ticket to fly home from Paris, he could afford to pay for some classes for me."

"Oh, Mom. That's so wrong. You deserve to do what you want now. You raised five kids. It's your turn to accomplish something of your own," I urged her. "Tell Dad you're doing it anyway. Take the money out of your joint account. Just do it."

"It's too late, Susie," came my mommy's tranquilized, foggy voice. "He burned the books."

"He what? Daddy did what?"

"Right there. In the fireplace. In front of the boys. He said he didn't want me leaving the house. Doing things on my own. One by one, he tore up my books and chucked them into the blaze," she said. "I had to give up the idea of going to college. It was too upsetting for Daddy."

Elva stood up and cleared the breakfast dishes. I gaped at the clumsy, woodsy mural that had been painted by the previous tenant on the living room wall.

I sighed.

More and more I knew why I had left home at twenty-two and never returned. The old Buffalo, New York oppression was alive and well and living in Elm Grove, Wisconsin. As I sat there making circles on the tablecloth with my bitten index fingertip, I suddenly remembered how my Dad had to have three spoons and extra plates for his salad and bread at every meal. Setting his princely place at the end of the table annoyed the table-setting child I was. "Why does Daddy get to have three spoons and two extra plates?" I had asked her.

"Because, Honey, men are essential."

After two more uneasy months in white bread, manicured Elm Grove, Wisconsin, I simply had to escape. My despairing mother's very presence, her endless naps and the pint bottle of whiskey crouching behind the anti-depressants in the kitchen cupboard spooked me. Nobody mentioned Elva's illness. Everybody tiptoed. My long-lost mommy had become the elephant in her own drawing room.

At summer's end, the Lion and the Rooster chipped in and bought me a one-way ticket out of their hair and back to Paris. I had exactly forty dollars in cash and a few hundred in traveler's checks in my purse. Yet, broke as I was, in Paris I felt refreshed and comforted. My eyes were regaled by the open markets' alluring pyramids of fruits and vegetables, guaranteed pre-mauled by human hands. In Paris, well-dressed, poised pedestrians strutted the streets, and Gustave Eiffel's folly was right where had I left it, defying gravity forever. Here I felt that powerful permanence that even the Nazis had declined to destroy. Millions of dead French bodies slept beneath my feet. Their very presence grounded me.

I had been collaborating with the enemy for too long. My life, thus far, had been but a dress rehearsal for the role of star bulldozer in my own personal urban-renewal project. Ever so cautiously now, I would push the muck of the past into monumental heaps, then demolish them at my own rate. On my terms.

From a modest-priced garret room in L'Hôtel Franklin Roosevelt on the *rue Clement-Marot*, I plotted to begin my new life by reviving my sleeping prince, Xavier Faure de la Taille. I rang him up. "Allo, Xavier."

"Who is on the apparatus?" Xavier asked. In those days in France, that was the classic answer-the-phone question. Everybody called the telephone *l'appareil* or the apparatus. In any case, Xavier mistrusted the phone. You never knew who might call. It could be someone from beneath your social class.

"It's Suzanne. *C'est moi. Comment ça va?*"

"Is that really you?" Xavier was wary of strangers.

"Yes. It's me. Susie Hoskins. Remember?"

"It's really you?

"No, it's Marie Antoinette. I'm calling about the cake."

"Oh. It *is* you."

"I'd like to invite you to lunch," I said.

"Where?" he asked.

"I don't care. You can choose. Meet me at the Franklin Roosevelt Hôtel at one o'clock."

He agreed. I knew he would. In French to invite someone to lunch or dinner means the bill is on you. Xavier fancied being invited.

Having brought along only a few hundred dollars, the one thing I needed more urgently than a lover was a good job. I went out to buy the Herald Tribune — for the classifieds. I passed the uppity Hôtel Plaza Athenée and made my way through feather-dusting chauffeurs and their respective "For Hire" Rolls-Royces. *Paris is indeed a nice place to live*, I mused, *but costly to visit*. I sat down with my newspaper on a café terrace near the Champs-Elysées.

The want ads were discouraging. It was late summer. Paris empties out in summer. Work stops. Every self-respecting Parisian goes on holiday. Hence, no jobs were available at the international firms that usually hired bilingual secretaries. I folded the paper and took the long way back to my hotel, window-shopping the expensive *couture* boutiques in the Avenue Montaigne. Dior's painted front was like French Wedgwood. Not blue with white trim. Sedate gray with white trim. Chic. Elegant. Appetizing. *One day when I'm rich*, I told myself, *I will be able to buy an haute couture frock.*

I walked along the *rue Marbeuf*, glanced up and noticed a billowing

American flag hanging from a freshly sandblasted stone facade. At first sight, I wondered if the flag flew from the apartment of some extra patriotic expatriate Yankee. But then I read the plaque beside the door of the be-flagged building. It said USAF Europe. Of course! The US armed forces were stationed here. Underneath the plaque was a notice: Personnel Offices. *1er étage.*

Two at a time, I mounted the steps to the first floor. Breathless, I burst through the door. "May I please see the personnel manager?"

Everything in the office, including the Pillsbury Dough Girl secretary, was drab, pale and lifeless, the desks were metal, the walls painted institutional green.

"The director is occupied," said the pallid lady. Her accent was civil servant mid-Atlantic stateside flat.

"I'll wait." I sat down on a green chair.

The secretary said, "Here. Take four copies of Form 57B, three copies of Form 57C and one of 57E. Fill them out and come back at three o'clock."

Determined not to budge from my seat, I leaned over to accept the forms from her. I leafed through them. It would have taken three days to fill in all the blanks. There was a lot the United States government needed to know about a possible employee: Father's mother's maiden name, great-grandmother's country of birth, itemized list of Christmas presents received in chronological order since World War II, etc., etc.

A door opened to emit a portly Black gentleman in a plaid sports jacket, too-short pants and brilliant white socks inside of shiny cordovan wingtips. "Got any more?" he asked the secretary.

"There's only me!" I rose and shook my forms at him.

Astonished, the man faced me, looked my own form up and down and asked, "And who, my dear, is 'me'?"

"My name is Susan Lee Hoskins. I am a certified schoolteacher. My French is perfect. I can sing, dance and even type a little when pushed." Lashes aflutter, I slipped him some skin, curtsying politely in case he preferred manners to gall.

"Howard Brothers," he said, introducing himself. "I'm the personnel director for the French theater of operations. Teaching positions are scarce around here," he said, seating his affable self behind a random metal desk and bade me sit opposite. "You see, Miss Hoskins, almost every American teaching applicant wants to live and work in France. They know they can draw their salary in strong Yankee dollars and soak up the French *joie de vivre* that we are all so fond of. Unfortunately, there's not much I can offer you here in France. I could probably find you something in Germany. Would you like to go teach in Frankfurt?"

"Not unless the French deport me," I said.

Brothers ran a finger up and down the list of available civil service positions. "There is one thing here," he said, looking up at me. "But you would hate it."

I crossed my legs fetchingly. "Don't be so sure. I push a mean broom." I threw him my most engaging "class clown" grin.

"It's a terrible job," he warned. "Teacher/counselor in a high school full of army brats. The base is about fifty miles from Paris in Bleaksville." He smiled back at me.

I knew Brothers liked me. "Where's Bleaksville?" I laughed.

"Ever been to Kansas?" he asked. "This place looks like Kansas in the rain. It's wet, windy and, well... it's bleak. I have only been to the school on this particular base once — on an inspection tour. It's France's answer to Siberia. The school is isolated. The nearest town is twelve miles away. It's called Dreux."

"Isn't that in Normandy?"

"Not if Normandy has anything to say about it. The air base in question is situated smack in the middle of hundreds of flat kilometers of yellow wheat fields. It's called *La Beauce*. Not exactly a tourist attraction," he chuckled. "How's your psych?"

"Excellent!" I lied.

"The job is unusual," Brothers explained. "Are you married?"

"Not at the moment."

"Good! Because these teacher/counselors I speak of have to sleep in a dormitory with ninety teen-aged girls for seven straight nights. Then they get seven well-earned days off. Most people go bats."

"You mean I would get seven days off every other week? What's the salary?" I asked.

"Six thousand and PX privileges. Take my word for it, Miss Susan

Lee Hoskins, this is a rough assignment. The only reason there's an opening now is that all three people who had the job last year had nervous breakdowns and had to be flown back to the States."

I signed on, sight unseen, to the role of surrogate mom, shrink, mother confessor and nursemaid to swarms of boarded adolescent government dependents. I calculated rapidly in my head. Six thousand dollars worth of francs was a fortune in France in those days. And, with all those weeks off, including school holidays, I would only be working twenty weeks a year! Bliss. I leapt from my chair, ran around the desk and hugged Howard Brothers. "Mr. Brothers, sir, honey, darling, cutie-poops, lambykins," I smacked him a kiss on his smooth ebony cheek. "You just call me Susie. Ya hear? Jes' plain Susie."

Through the milling early lunchtime crowds, I raced back to my hotel to dress. In the excitement, any hesitation I had about what to wear to the reunion with Xavier was forgotten. I hastily donned a red cotton full skirt and frilly white blouse that I found near the top of my suitcase. I grabbed a sweater, checked my watch and took the elevator down to greet my past.

Gloved and be-suited, as always, Xavier resembled a shabby peacock in full array. He puffed himself up a bit more before kissing me on both cheeks. In turn, I planted a warm kiss on his mouth. He recoiled and stood back to scrutinize my appearance. "You look very American," he hissed.

I put last year's limbo of navy blue and gray curtsies soundly behind me and said, "And you look like a portrait of your own grandfather," I went on, "Wouldn't you be more comfortable if you took off that heavy suit of blue serge armor?"

"Same old Suzanne," he smirked.

Xavier had decided he wanted lunch at our former haunt, *Chez Francis*. While we were walking there, I was calculating which wine I would order to cushion the flow of empty small talk Xavier kept spewing. He told me that his sister's new baby had come out five pounds and only a girl. Great family chagrin. No direct heir. He deplored his rich aunt's clean bill of health. He griped about the law exams he had failed because he didn't respect France's modern legal innovations. Not a word of, "Hi, honey. How are you?" found its way out of his mouth.

No matter how much we had bickered, in my heart of hearts Xavier was still my Frog Prince, my knight in a shiny blue serge blazer. "Did you miss me?" I wondered.

"Not all the time," he said.

He used to love me so much, I thought, *all the time.* As we walked along, Xavier didn't take my hand. Why was he keeping his distance? My prince had repeatedly assured me that he loved me. He wrote me mushy letters from France all the way to Wisconsin. But now, here in Paris, I was too American. Too cheeky. Too loud. Too Red, White and Blue. Not Blue, White and Red enough.

At *Chez Francis,* the gallant *maître d'hôtel* seated us. He remembered me. He said it was good to see that *mademoiselle* was back in Paris. I ordered an extra fine bottle of wine. It came directly. Xavier sniffed and tested it. And, as he was not paying the bill, he nodded to the waiter to pour.

I was proud of having landed a job and bragged a bit to Xavier about my unusual hiring experience that morning in *la rue Marbeuf.* "Soon I will be making enough money to buy a car," I enthused. Xavier said he disapproved of girls driving automobiles. "They make hysterical decisions and are a menace to other drivers." I changed the subject.

Rather than try to oppose Xavier's strong opinions, I hailed the *maître d'hôtel.* "Jeannot, please bring us the menu," I said, and tapped on the nearly empty wine bottle, indicating the need for seconds.

"You drink too much." Xavier was at me again.

"I certainly do," I smiled and accepted the menu from Jeannot, who leaned over discreetly to say, "If *monsieur* does not mind, I offer you a second bottle of wine as a welcome home to Paris." Informing Jeannot that the lunch was on me would only have deepened Xavier's scowl. I accepted Jeannot's *beau geste* with a girlish smile and added, *"Merci Jeannot. Vous êtes trop gentil."*

Xavier sucked in a noble breath. "Suzanne," he then intoned, "I'm afraid I still love you." This declaration was delivered as though from a vending machine. Flat. Monotone. Expressionless.

Surprised, I pondered this unanticipated news. *How could he still love me and be so cold to me?* It took me a minute or two to wake up to the fact that I found myself in a classic romantic bind. *Get yourself on your feet. Find a good job. Threaten to buy your own transportation. Throw a few free meals their way. And presto! They are,* "afraid they still love you." Xavier *still loved me*. Why? Because I was going to have a job and he was not. Working, I recalled, was not correct for people of his social status.

It was irritating to realize that all my own successes were finally due to some mammoth masculine loan society. Whatever I wanted to do in life, I had to apply for the privilege from men. "*Merde!*" I mumbled behind my tall menu. "If you love me, Xavier," I came out of hiding to say, "then why the hell don't you even like me?" I placed the *carte* next to my plate as a signal to Jeannot that we were ready to order.

"Because I only love you."

Xavier knew I preferred the heel of the bread to munch on. He retrieved the end piece of baguette from the breadbasket and handed it to me. He poured me more wine, looking straight into my eyes so I couldn't help but see the stars in his.

To seduce, he would stoop to giving up the crunchiest bit of bread. *My ass, you love me, chéri,* I confided to myself.

We ate our lunch in separate silences, Xavier, misty-eyed and a smidgeon too tipsy to trust his loosened tongue. As for me, I held my tongue and used it to gobble the scrumptious *gigot aux flageolets* as though it would be my last chance at lamb in any form in this lifetime.

Even before spearing the last bite, I waved to Jeannot and mouthed the magic word, *dessert*. French food only made me hungrier for more French food. Jeannot hurried off to fetch the dessert trolley. Professional *garçons* had a sixth sense about famished foreign females.

The Peach Melba with Chantilly cream was my choice. It was and still is my most vivid culinary *souvenir* from *Chez Francis*. Xavier dabbed at his chin with his napkin, saying, "You have gained a few kilos, *non*?"

"You're right! *Non*," I snapped at him across the table. The waiter served me a frosted silver cup where two peach halves hugged a pyramid of vanilla ice cream. A dollop of currant jelly trickled in all directions down the ice cream's mountainside. I might have even slurped as I vacuum-cleaned my plate, enjoying myself, despite the haughty sighs floating over Xavier's cognac snifter.

"Suzanne," he moaned, "please stop that."

I laid my sticky spoon on the cleanest part of the linen tablecloth. "Stop what? Stop eating as though I enjoy it? Stop talking to lowly waiters as though they were my equals? Stop being flattered because

Jeannot likes me? Stop laughing and whistling in the streets?" Xavier nodded. He thought I was getting his point and patted the air vigorously to remind me to quiet down.

"*Non*, Xavier. I won't quiet down. *Non*. *Non*. And *non* again." I raised my eyes to meet his. "I have come back to Paris to live my life. My way. If you love me so much, how come you can't stand the sight of me? What is it that frightens you so? Did your parish priest warn you about those good-time ration cards we have to turn in on Judgment Day? 'Sorry, sir, too many chuckle holes punched in yours. Go wait in the Purgatory line. I regret, *Monsieur*, you have used up all your tickle credits. Straight to Hell.' Why don't you spoil yourself a little, Xavier? Have another cognac. Then go home and play with yourself!" I scribbled in the air for Jeannot to bring the bill. "And please bring another cognac for *monsieur* and make that one for me as well."

"You are incorrigible," Xavier muttered. He did not refuse the second brandy. "And your nails are all bitten down again."

I didn't take time to savor my cognac. In one gulp I finished half the glass and paid the bill. I wriggled sexily against Jeannot as he helped me into my cardigan sweater. "The state of my fingernails," I remarked to Xavier, "will never have to disgust you again." Whetting my whistle with the last of my Rémy Martin, I left the restaurant tootling *The Star-Spangled Banner* and throwing kisses to the kitchen staff.

I did pause to kiss Xavier goodbye. Two chilly kisses, one on each cheek. I was weary of conforming to that biblical crap about sowing the wind and reaping the whirlwind. I *was* the whirlwind.

CHAPTER FOURTEEN

F rench people were dismayed about Kennedy's death. They approached any and every American within kissing distance, grabbed their hands in theirs and with a lugubrious grimace said, *"Oh Mon dieu, Mon dieu, Mon dieu, je suis désolée."* By the very looks on their faces, we Americans knew that they meant, *"My god, my god, my god, I am desolate."* Not all the Americans the French stopped on the street to commiserate with actually understood the *desolate* part. But little matter, it's the thought that counts.

As for me, I had liked Kennedy. I cried. A lot. But I was a dormitory counselor. A substitute parent. I couldn't cry in front of the kids. So, for their sake, I endeavored to appear composed. They, on the contrary, went nuts. The assassination had brought their hysteria level to a rare pitch. Directly we heard the news, our students commenced falling about. If they'd been standing, they slid down the wall, sprawled on the floor and rapidly went weepy bonkers insane. Or they lay on their beds prostrate and dumb, fearing that the president's disappearance meant war. Their fathers would be called up and what was worse, they themselves would have to ship back to live at home with their families in Texas or Arkansas, somewhere in a tacky trailer on a real American military base in America.

Of course they were worried their fathers might be stationed far away and even that they might never come home. But they were teenagers. Foremost in their collective mind was their own fate. They cried because they would miss France and Dreux Air Force Base. No more late-night sneaks for the purpose of giggling till they couldn't breathe — all the while puffing on forbidden cigarettes. No more Rec Center dances with music blasting, free snacks and sodas. Living back in the States would mean the end of illicit snogs in empty dorm rooms. And *sob sob* there would be no more bus trips to *Mont St Michel*, shopping jaunts to the vast PX in *Belmanoir* near Paris or actual field trips to the gracious, elegant, stylish city of Paris itself where they even sometimes got to sleep overnight in comfy French hotels. The girls knew that the sumptuous perks they had enjoyed during all of the halcyon last years of their fathers' service to peacekeeping in Europe had been paid for by the king. Now the king was dead.

Life went on. I drove in and out of Paris. I saw Xavier sometimes. Made love once in a while. We often argued in the car. As a matter of conversation, I remember saying, "The world will be a better place when everybody is beige or brown or something different. Not just white."

Xavier retorted. "Only a fool would make such a vapid remark."

I was insulted. I made him get out of the car and walk home or take a bus, or, God forbid, the Métro.

More and more I realized that I might have to give up my dream of being married to Xavier in favor of my so far futile quest for an authentic, realistic man of my dreams. Xavier's luster and my lust for his scrawny sweet self had all but worn off. Did I cheat on Xavier? Well, yes I did. Often with high society gentlemen and dishy, fashion plate guys or a man I might meet at the Café Flore or Les Deux Magots in Saint Germain des Près. Paris was crawling with eligible enthusiastic lovers. Free Love seemed to have been born there.

Moreover, I was twenty-five years old and still hadn't experienced a real man to woman orgasm. All the men I had slept with — bar none — had been pumpers. They made love to me vigorously, groaning with pleasure, turning red, swelling the veins in their foreheads, sweating and wearing themselves to a frazzle. Despite all the energy they expended, I felt nothing. Slippery? Yes. And sexually aroused. But invariably I would be left in the orgasm lurch. My occasional lovers worked so hard at their earnest thrustings that I often wondered if they were trying to inflate me.

A young person who read the pre-publication manuscript of this book asked me, "How can you explain the promiscuity? Was it French?"

"No," I explained. "It was not entirely French. Not really. It was simply the spirit of the mad Sixties. We were, back then, what my mother might have called 'loose' and it was sublimely amusing."

The flimsy paper wall calendars we received from *La Poste* in exchange for a tip to the postman were always topped by a beatific image of baby lambs suckling or the swaddled infant Jesus and his virgin mother Mary. We could choose: Lambs or Jesus. Mine boasted three lambkins and their wooly mom standing in a field in Normandy. The calendar revealed it was 1963. But nobody young and free like myself in Paris had a clue that it was indeed The Swinging Sixties. It was just our Parisian life as usual.

In my day, there was nobody to ask about my non-orgasmic dilemma. I'd have been too shy to discuss it with a friend, too embarrassed to ask any doctor and surely not considered a possible girlfriend by any man I might confess it to. I was confused. Xavier was my official boyfriend. Our lovemaking had remained lukewarm. So I kept trying out new gentlemen hoping one might give me an orgasm whilst making love. As it was, when the man would come away from his exertions heaving, perspiring as though he had just jogged eight miles, he would grab a cigarette, lie back on the pillows and ask, "How was it for you?"

If I had managed to fake a convincing orgasm, I'd swoon his way, take a fake drag off his cigarette and sigh, "*Fantastique.*" If, however, I had felt nothing and had instead monitored the guy's ceaseless plunges in hopes he wouldn't die on me, I'd mumble some lie like "*merveilleux*" or "*excellent*" and turn over and go to sleep. Many times, I would simply get back into my clothes, find a taxi and sashay on home where I went on wondering to myself if I was malformed — if all the diddling and fingerings I had put my pussy through since I was barely old enough to whistle had rendered my private parts numb.

In other words, in Paris in the Sixties, sexual congress with almost anyone you might meet in a café was naughty but acceptable. Socially and morally, sex was part of life. You started young and never stopped. In summer, Parisian parents went off to the seaside with the younger children and left their teenagers behind. While their folks were away, fifteen- and sixteen-year-olds made all manner of whoopee in their parents' apartments — all the while being cautious not to topple Grandmother's Sèvres *soupière* or soil the Louis Quinze settee. Antique treasures with historical value were to be preserved and passed on to your children. But in France, your sex life was a private matter. It was not something you hung on to so as to bequeath it to the next generation.

In the United States, where I was from, such tiptoe subjects as sex were rarely, if ever, discussed. And back there, too often one used the words should and shouldn't to refer to what God or Jesus might think if you did consummate a flirtation. Conversely, sex in France was like eating. You did it because you found the dish appealing, you were hungry and it felt good.

I was fairly certain that other women I knew had orgasms whilst making love. Especially French women who would always give you a report on this man or that who was either *"une bonne affaire"* or *"la plus mauvaise affaire sur la place de Paris."* For my French girlfriends, the men they slept with were either a good bargain or the worst bargain in all of Paris.

My *copines'* ruthless labeling of their conquests did not, however, give me much insight into the purely technical aspects of sexual contact with men. Was I a failure? A sexual loser? A love cripple? Whatever I was, I was an utter washout in the man-woman orgasm department. If I wasn't, then why did I have to scrub my clit to climax in the bathroom after Jacques or Pierre or Jean-Louis had smeared the sheets and my innards with their ejections?

Shortly after the Christmas Kennedy died, I began experiencing frequent stomachaches. The young doctor on the base where I worked had told me he was not there to diagnose stomachaches. "I am here to stay out of Vietnam," he said. To his credit, he did push and pinch and prod at my stomach. But he found nothing exciting and sent me packing.

I wondered if I might be pregnant. I had never used birth control much. I owned a diaphragm. But that device squeezed my bladder in a painful place. I often resisted wearing it. Then one day a Cockney girl I met at a party in Montparnasse said, "Honey, your pessary don't work if you leave it in the top drawer." She called my diaphragm by a funny name. But I nonetheless gathered she meant the painful rubber disk that I avoided using. From then on, I tried to remember to insert the damned diaphragm every day. Then I'd forget and have a fling and then worry myself into a lather. A few weeks later, I would get my period and go back to being cavalier about birth control. Even with all my rollings about in various hays with an impressive bevy of gentlemen callers, my body forgot to get pregnant.

The tummy aches came and went. I didn't have a fever. I didn't throw up. But there was definitely recurrent pain in my lower right side. I finally gave in and went to a French doctor who diagnosed me with chronic appendicitis. Was there even such an illness?

Dr. Rondouillard was oldish, whiskery and chubs. But he had come highly recommended by my friend Madame Ratier about whom I will wax and gush a bit later. Marguerite Ratier only frequented the best and the brightest Parisian specialists. She made me an appointment. It was decided then and there. I would have my appendix removed. Madame Ratier's chauffeur drove me to her favorite *Clinique* in Neuilly, Paris's closest, poshest suburb.

In France, hospitals are big, not very tall, meandering, public, well-landscaped and run by the government health plan. *Cliniques* are smaller, more intimate and private. These latter establishments have often been carved out of old mansions commonly referred to as *hôtels particuliers.* Their labyrinthine stairways and wrought iron-encased elevators impressed one as home-like and cozy. *Cliniques* were the un-hospitals. The overall clinique ambiance was chic and even charming. Sheets were pink. Pillowcases stark white and ruffled. Nurses elegantly attired in *couture* uniforms. *Cliniques* to this day are for both caring for the sick and for making money. Hospitals are for caring for the sick for almost free and keeping patients there for as long as they need to be looked after. *Cliniques* are for caring for or operating on people for a price and then charging a pretty penny to keep them there as long as the *clinique* can legally suck on their bank accounts. The quality of care in each type of facility is equal. It is, however, considered more academically prestigious for a doctor to work in the public sector. And the public hospital usually has better food. Having no choice between the two, I was sedated and rolled into the very private upscale Wedgwood blue operating theater in the basement of *La Clinique des Lilas.*

Dr Rondouillard looked quite astonishing in his surgical mask. Errant white curly hairs protruded from its sides. He looked as though he was attempting to conceal a Santa Claus costume. That silly image of Dr. Rondouillard's maverick whiskers wriggling out from the sides of his surgical mask lasted but seconds before I was asleep. When I awoke my appendix was gone. I was on hold for food. But they gave me delicious broth and a *biscotte* to soak by dunking in the soup so the cracker wouldn't gag me on its way down. The pain was bearable, the personnel helpful and efficient.

Next morning, I was running a fever. Now armies of nurses filed in and out with hypodermic syringes. They drew vials of my blood and sent it down for analysis. The doctors came in groups. They looked puzzled, whispered and stroked their chins or caressed their beards. The nurses hooked me up to IVs and blood pressure gizmos that squeezed my arm every fifteen minutes. Apparently, from the sudden rush to my bedside of everything from aides to surgeons, I was really quite ill: jaundiced, feverish and nauseated. I, in fact, had hepatitis.

CHAPTER FIFTEEN

H epatitis had come calling on me once before. At age seven, I had gone all yellow on the parents. I missed the second grade. In each case, a badly sterilized needle had been the cause. Nobody sued anybody either time. My parents paid for the first jaundice and, with the kind participation of Marguerite Ratier, I paid for the second.

Who was Marguerite Ratier and how did I know her? While I was still working for Monsieur Traub in Paris in 1962, I received a call from a French friend. His name was Jacques Veit. As a summer job, Jacques was interning at *La Sorbonne.* He had been to university in the States so when anyone called the *Sorbonne's* switchboard asking to talk to a person who spoke some English, Jacques had taken the call. That particular phone call was from Marguerite Ratier, a French woman who spoke no English. Marguerite had visited New York the year before with her daughter and, although they knew some British English, they could neither understand what was being said nor make themselves understood in NewYork. Marguerite and her grown-up daughter intended to make further visits to the US. They desperately needed an American English teacher. Where best to call to find an American teacher but the French university? Had it been you or I, we'd probably have rung up the US Embassy. Not Marguerite. She was French. My good friend Jacques suggested they meet with me. Marguerite rang me at the office. I agreed to meet with her and her daughter the next day after work. They would come fetch me in front of Traub's office building at 8 rue Clément-Marot at six p.m.

I expected to meet an oldish lady and her perky younger daughter. Quite the opposite. I was picked up that evening in a chauffeured black Citröen DS —pronounced: day yes — by perky, elegant fifty-year-old Marguerite and her starchy young daughter, Paulette. Marguerite, it turned out, was a wealthy widow who lived alone with her timid, intellectual daughter and her pious, senior citizen mother in a mansion in the fashionable Paris suburban neighborhood of Parc de Sceaux. Marguerite directed Monsieur Robert, her chauffeur — a retired police officer — to take us all to tea at Angelina near La Madeleine. Over tea and *petits fours* we decided on a schedule for the Ratiers' English lessons. From that day forward, Marguerite sent Monsieur Robert to fetch me every Saturday morning at nine. It was a bit of a drive to Sceaux. Maybe twenty-five, thirty minutes, depending on traffic. Years went by and I never got a word out of Monsieur Robert beyond *Bonjour Mademoiselle* and *au revoir* to the same *Mademoiselle*. Then one day Robert died. He was replaced by a handsome whippersnapper named Fred whom I never liked. He talked incessantly — about himself. And he did not call me *Mademoiselle*. He used Suzanne.

Robert drove the big black Citroën DS — the kind with hissing hydraulic ups and downs — to the Ratier house without incident. Marguerite, Paulette and I used TIME magazine as our textbook. Each week I assigned an article. Next week we discussed it in English. We were getting to know each other and one fine day Marguerite invited me to stay on past the morning for *le déjeuner* — lunch. The Ratier dining room was grand. Glasses were crystal. Table cutlery was golden *vermeil*. It was during one of these succulent midday meals that I learned that the ringing I kept hearing was not the back doorbell. A pedal at Marguerite's foot beneath the Persian rug under the vast dining table was used to ring the bell to call the servant to bring the next course.

For me, the American teacher girl from Buffalo, those weekly visits to the Ratiers' house represented total immersion in the French *bourgeois* lifestyle. *Bourgeois* means neither peasant nor noble in French. This social class label is more like what Americans think of as the moneyed middle class. Bourgeois people don't have titles and usually have newish money. They *buy* chateaux and renovate them. The noble families *inherit* them and leave them to crumble. It was at the Ratiers' that I learned which forks and what knives and spoons were for what and when. It was there they taught me to make *crème caramel* and *gratin de pommes de terre*. And after lunch, out of hearing distance of Paulette, Marguerite would confide the secrets of her numerous paramours. I was rapt.

Little by little we all three became accustomed to one another. Marguerite and I got on like neighboring houses afire. Paulette was a tad reticent. Her idea of what young women our age ought to be doing with their lives was different from mine. Paulette was three years older than me. She had the equivalent of an MBA from the prestigious business school HEC in Paris. She had been the sole female graduate that year. Paulette had, moreover, been tied into straitlaced knots by her grandmother, Hermine Decombeix. By the time I met her, Hermine was in her early seventies. She was a spry and domineering dragon of a woman who had been born before the turn of the 20th century. Hermine had lived through both wars and had always managed largely on her own. At some point she had agreed to come live with her daughter Marguerite and her granddaughter, Paulette, in the mansion in *Le Parc de Sceaux*.

Having been widowed by the first World War, Hermine was obliged to provide for herself and her daughter. After losing her husband she had continued to run their grocery/café business in the remote Auvergne. Even after she had married Marguerite off to the Ratier wealth, Hermine carried on working hard in her shop. Later, during the second World War, living in Paris became dangerous. For safety's sake, Marguerite shipped Paulette down to the Auvergne to live with strictly Catholic Hermine, attend religious school and dress in the sober navy blue and gray manner befitting a girl of her background. Hence the pious tinge to Paulette's loving but suspicious personality.

Marguerite's wealthy father-in-law, Monsieur Ratier senior, was a typical Auvergnat — tight-fisted and dour. Ratier was an aeronautical genius. He had invented the variable pitch propeller. War had made him rich. By the time Marguerite married his younger son in 1933, Monsieur Ratier senior was gigantically rich. He lived most of the time near his factory in Figeac, a remote bustling town in the coldest central part of France. But for business purposes, he kept a house and a branch of his factory just south of Paris in the near suburban town of Chatillon. Chatillon is close by the 14th arrondissement, which was at the time the *Auvergnat* neighborhood in town.

It was the custom in Paris in the early part of the 20th century for *Auvergnat* fathers to seek suitable wives for their sons among their own kind. In turn, savvy *Auvergnat* mothers presented their daughters to the old geezers for their approval. Much of this wife trading happened in the local headquarters of the people from Auvergne, which was called La Brasserie Zeyer. It still exists today. You will find it catty-corner across from the church of Saint Pierre de Montrouge at La Place d'Alésia. Order the *Chateaubriand sauce Béarnaise*.

Marguerite was but sixteen when the savvy Hermine sent her off to Austria to a swanky finishing school. There, Marguerite had learned German, curtsying and proper manners. When she got back from Austria, her mother hastily gussied her up and took her to Paris to meet Monsieur Ratier. The old man was impressed. Marguerite was not only a beautiful, sturdy young woman, she had remarkable social graces. And she spoke German — a skill uncommon among the idle young women from the Auvergne who usually stayed at home, clumsily tinkling the ivories or sitting by the fireside embellishing their interminable embroidery projects. Out of all the girls he had considered for marriage to his youngest son, Marguerite was clearly the prize. It was all set. Marguerite would marry young Joseph Ratier whom she had never so much as glimpsed in a crowd.

Weeks later, upon invitation, Hermine Decombeix brought her daughter, Marguerite, clad in her Sunday best, by train to a chic hotel in Deauville in Normandy by-the-sea. Monsieur Ratier senior was throwing the lucky young couple a lavish engagement party. There, in a vast ballroom with hundreds of guests all dressed to the nines and awash in champagne, Monsieur Ratier senior slid the biggest diamond ring I have ever seen on Marguerite's pretty young finger.

Still, she had not met her future husband. Emboldened by the very weight of the giant bauble on her hand, she dared ask, "Where is Joseph?" The old man replied that his son would be down shortly. He was having a bath.

From that day forward, Marguerite was captive. A bird in a gilded cage. She married the flaccid, unappealing Joseph whose mustaches were so poorly aligned as to make him look slightly mad or un-balanced. His nose was a beak. He was dark, thin, small, haughty and nervous. Joseph was the youngest son of a powerful patriarch and brother to a handsome, egomaniacal, older sibling whose intentions were to keep his younger brother forever in the shadow and take over his father's thriving aircraft company. The couple's honeymoon took place in Venice. They traveled first class in a private compartment. Marguerite loved Venice. Joseph hated every minute. "Italy gives me indigestion," he had said.

But this is not Marguerite's story. It's mine. However, her life and mine were so closely allied for such a long time that we often spoke the same words at the same moment. Or we wore light blue on the same day without previous notice. Much of what I hadn't learned from my mother about life and how to live it, I was learning from Marguerite Ratier, a kindred spirit.

After the fever went down and the mustard color had somewhat faded from my skin, I was released from the *clinique*. I stayed a day or two in Paris with an American colleague who worked with me at Dreux. But she only had a small studio apartment. I had to find a place to live in the city to be near the doctors. I placed an ad on the bulletin board at the American Church on the Quai D'Orsay. "Inside Paris proper. Young American Teacher wants to share apartment with same." I must have given a phone number, but I don't recall which one or to whom it belonged. I certainly didn't have a phone. Nobody much did.

A quick reply came on the church bulletin board next day. It was from a thirtyish American lady who worked in the office at the military base called Belmanoir outside Paris. Her name was Shirley. Shirley had found a furnished apartment in the 17th arrondissement and needed someone to share the rent. I went there, took a look and agreed. She got the bedroom. I got the living room. In between us there was a corridor off which darted a tiny, dingy, yellowed bathroom, a separate WC and a teensy kitchen. The entry door was mid-hallway. So we didn't get in each other's way.

After ten days, I was beginning to actually feel somewhat better. And I was getting antsy. One morning, as I stood examining my still yellowish eyes in the mirror, it struck me that with but one can of white, I could repaint those dirty bathroom walls in a day. Those faded walls reminded me of my lemon-hued skin. If I got right to it, I would surprise my roommate. When she got home that evening the bathroom would be spanking fresh white.

So I went out, got the paint and brushes at the nearby *droguerie* — mini hardware store — and set up the stepladder to begin the job. For about two hours straight I painted and daubed and painted and wiped off paint, got up and down from the ladder and taped the woodwork edges and then painted some more.

Then I fainted.

When she got home after work, my roommate stumbled across me lying in the tub, yelped a good loud yelp and called down to the *concierge* to get the rescue squad. Her shriek had awakened me. By the time they got there, I was completely conscious. The paramedics had voted to bundle me off to the emergency room. I sat up in the middle of the hubbub and politely begged to be put back in my bed. How would Xavier ever find me if he scaled the wall of the French army base where he was stationed and sneaked into Paris to see me again? Without phones he had no way of alerting me to his visits. Our occasional tender moments and his companionship had become necessary to my flagging spirit. The rescuers complied with my wishes and slid me back under my covers.

My most faithful visitor was Marguerite Ratier. She came in from Sceaux every day. Her chauffeur would trudge up three floors to bring me homemade vegetable broth, bread, jam and flowers. Sometimes Marguerite would stop off at Fauchon or Ladurée and fetch me some exquisite *pâtes de fruits* which are flat, square gumdrop candies made only of the finest ingredients and fresh fruits. She would often send up a note with Monsieur Robert. "Don't worry, *chérie,*" she might say. "*Pâtes de fruits* are good for the liver." Her sweet notes reminded me that when I had come down with hepatitis at age seven, the remedy for a swift cure had been penicillin shots, lollipops, Jell-O and daily eggnogs with lots of sugar.

By the end of February, I was well enough to go back to work at the air base in Dreux. We still worked a week on and a week off, so I kept my room at Shirley's, but only used it half the time. I had a lot more money now. As a dormitory counselor I had to have a US teaching credential. As such I was considered both a civil servant and an officer. I was paid for sick leave. As I got stronger and regained some of my senses, I realized with no little trepidation that I would soon be obliged to either break it off with Xavier or convince him to come back to the States and marry me. As I have said before, I loved him. But I couldn't stand him. Besides, Marguerite hated him. He had come to lunch at the Ratiers' once on a Saturday. He'd brought a dolled up, beribboned velour box of chocolates from La Marquise de Sévigné — *the* chocolate boutique where only the best people shopped. Marguerite did not gush. She thanked him curtly, shook his hand and passed the box along to Hermine saying, "*Maman,* please take Monsieur's gift to the kitchen." Marguerite couldn't bear Xavier's uppity way of speaking, his exaggerated nobleman manners or his gloves. Moreover, she was wary of what she termed "his shifty eyes."

Each week when I was in town, I would still have lunch at the Ratiers'. So far neither Marguerite nor Paulette had learned much additional English. But we soldiered on with our lessons, for which they continued to pay me 100 francs (twenty dollars) a week. When I still worked for Traub, 100 francs extra every week was a fortune. My salary there was 1000 black cash francs ($200 US) a month. But once I was working at the base, the extra twenty dollars was frosting on the cake.

By now I felt like part of the Ratier family. Sometimes I would discuss economics with Paulette or dance with Hermine in the kitchen while she sang old WWI ditties. But I always finished up my visit with a private powwow in the living room on the small chintz couch in front of the fire, swapping love stories with Marguerite.

Once she asked me flat out, "Are you thinking of marrying that Xavier person?"

I answered, "Yes."

"Don't," Marguerite warned. "Don't even imagine yourself part of that milieu. They will always look down on you. No matter how hard you try, they will snub you and make you a figure of ridicule."

"But I have known Xavier for two years. He doesn't snub me. His sisters both like me. They even invite me to their homes and serve me tea. I know Xavier loves me."

"He will be an unfaithful husband."

"What? My Xavier unfaithful? Never!" I said. "He's not like that Marguerite."

"They are all *like that*," she said. "Every man alive cheats on his wife. And your Xavier is a born skirt-chaser and moreover he's a gold digger. Look at his eyes. Once he realizes your family has no money back there in Meennysota or wherever you live, he will bolt. Do not count on Xavier for your future."

I was crushed. And angry. How could my dear friend Marguerite not adore my handsome young suitor? It was true that I couldn't stand his uppity ways or abide his stuffiness either. But if my girlish dream came true, once we were back in the United States, teaching French to well-heeled youngsters in private schools, Xavier would learn about our democracy and love thy neighbor and become accustomed to our ways. He would leave those pigskin gloves behind forever.

I didn't exit Marguerite's house in a huff that day, but I was hurt and so took off early to see *Citizen Kane* for the tenth time at the Cinémathèque in *la rue d'Ulm*.

Not long after Marguerite's warning, one evening before I dropped him off at his parents' place, Xavier stayed in the car, lit a Gauloise, sat back and murmured, all crestfallen and humble, "I am afraid I have made Chantal de Boudeville pregnant."

I gasped. Madame de Boudeville! The plump, fortyish wife of the old geezer who strode about puffing out his chest in the apartment next door to Xavier's parents.

"But, Suzanne," he reached over, patted my shoulder and said, "do not worry. I will not marry her." I didn't laugh or inquire further. I asked him to exit my automobile and drove on home where I wept bitter tears of regret. Could I have been so naïve? In a word, yes.

After his discomfiting revelation, Xavier wrote me letters and sent gifts and pleaded with me to understand. He had gone to confession and was doing penance and was truly sorry for what he had done. As for Marguerite, she was more than thrilled to see the back of the leather elbow patches on Xavier's brother's hand-me-down Harris tweed jacket. "He is no good. He's rotten. Those noble people feel they can get away with anything. So long as they go to confession and accept the priest's penance and repeat their Hail Marys a thousand times, they believe they are absolved. Then they carry on as usual. You are well rid of that young man, *ma chère. Bon débarras!* which of course means good riddance.

It was coming on Easter in 1964. My dorm counselor pal Suzanne Burke and I wanted to take a trip somewhere over the Easter vacation. One night we met up with a guy named Neil Phillips at the officers' club. Neil lived on base with his lovely wife Nancy, who worked as entertainment director at the base NCO recreation center. Except that he was married to the good Nancy, I never knew what Neil did around there. He wasn't a dorm counselor. Maybe he was a teacher. I didn't see much of the teachers. We dorm people were not located in the school proper and were not acquainted with all the people who worked there.

Once, at a school get-together that we were obliged to attend, I had to ask a fellow counselor, "Who is the little bald man with the tie? My question was met with a chuckle, "That's Al Matthews. The high school principal." Al Matthews was my boss.

Neil Phillips had had a few beers that evening and was holding forth about Ibiza. "It's such a cool place," he told us. "It's wild and natural. It's still really a peasant culture. Farms dot the countryside. Farmers still move their goods on mules. Ibiza's serene and bucolic. But now there are hundreds of foreigners there. All kinds. Germans and Americans, Dutch and English and even some Australians have gone to Ibiza to chill out."

Neil's use of our language was foreign to me. I wasn't sure what "cool" meant in his context. Ibiza was an island in the Mediterranean and so was reputedly warm. I certainly didn't know what it meant to go to a warm place to chill out. The very idea of chilling clashed with my tropical notion of the magical island Neil was raving about. I didn't know for sure. But I had a hunch that these new vocabulary words belonged to something Bohemian. Something like a cult or a special community of people I knew nothing about.

Sue Burke and I drove down to Ibiza in my own new car — a metallic blue Renault Gordini I had acquired thanks, once again, to the base branch of The Bank of America. I was exhausted. Yet I sped all the way down the Route Nationale 20, passing enticing places I had never yet seen. Orléans, Limoges and Brive and then, after I had hallucinated the Beatles' *Rubber Soul* album photo of the four boys' heads on the side of a cliff hanging over the road, I decided we'd better stop. I woke Suzanne, who had been curled up asleep in the back seat for the entire journey. We agreed to spend the night in Toulouse.

Right away when we got there, we were met by a pair of young university- type Toulouse boys who claimed they had been following us for many kilometers. Those clean-cut *Toulousain* boys fed us and took us dancing in a popular disco and then dropped us off at our hotel. Nice people. Great accent. I vowed I would come back some-day.

Next day we passed through Carcassonne and Perpignan and finally we crossed the border into Spain. The roads in Spain were trea-cherous. Rutted and pitted and gravelly dangerous. When we passed the town of Gerona we knew Barcelona could not be far. It was there we would catch the ferry next day to Ibiza. The Ibiza boat left from the port in front of the statue of Christopher Columbus. By the time we got to Barcelona, it was late afternoon. We needed a place to spend the night. Our funds were limited so we chose an upscale fleabag where there was, at least, a shower.

It was in that *pensión* in Barcelona that I met my most useful life-time lover. The telephone shower attachment.

CHAPTER SIXTEEN

While I was rinsing my private parts with the telephone shower attachment that evening in our rudimentary Barcelona pensión's bathroom, the surging water pressure hit my clit. You know that feeling when you discover something that is not new? Something you ought to have discovered years before? When you get that, 'Why didn't I think of that?' flash? Well, that shower attachment epiphany was just such a moment. If you are not European you may not even know what a telephone shower is. Envision a screw-in apparatus with a hose leading to a shower head. In French these are called *douches téléphones* and in many cases, there is no up-top shower. If you want water beating down on your head and body from up above, you hook the telephone shower to a vertical metal bar on the wall and slide it up to the height from which you desire to receive water on your head. Here, there was just the bathtub and this miracle, pre-cellular telephone device. It was screwed onto the top of the faucets. When applied to the right or left side of my clitoris for long enough, the jets from the telephone shower produced a nifty orgasm. That night in Barcelona's pensión de Familia Eulalia, I knew I had hit the jackpot.

No more fishing around for creams or lotions. No more concealing myself in locked bathrooms or cubbies in order to diddle myself to climax. From then on, I could just hop in the tub. Indeed, I have perpetually wondered how women do wash their genitalia in a standard up-top shower. And to this day, the mystery persists. Same with feet. Does a body stand on one leg to soap and rinse first left then right? Damn dangerous if you ask me. Vive la *douche téléphone*.

Ibiza. Today the very name of that hopping Balearic island screams *Disco*. When Suzanne Burke and I finally got there in April of 1964, there was no such thing as a disco — there or anywhere else. We had left the car at the Barcelona airport where guarded parking was but five cents a day. Then we went back to town in a taxi and boarded the big boat to Ibiza. Once at our destination, we found ourselves in a tiny Spanish town with a hotel in the center and few, if any, cars on the streets. The older women walked about town stopping to gossip or shop. They wore long black dresses with black or sometimes colored shawls draped as scarves over their heads. Cloth shoes similar to *éspadrilles* covered their feet. Their shawls fell around their shoulders and came to a point at the middle of their backs. Younger women might not wear the shawl over their hair, but would instead simply drape it around their shoulders. Almost all women sported a single long pigtail down the middle of their backs. Sometimes a bow graced the bottom of their braid. A few, perhaps privileged, rebellious or shopkeeper young women wore printed crepe dresses with high-heeled sandals à la WWII.

A German woman we had met on the big boat which had floated us for twelve bumpy hours to the magical island told us about a clean boarding house run by a German friend of hers. "There you will be safe," she told us and gave us the address. We took a taxi from the port to a beachfront area just outside of Ibiza town called Figueretas. There, we were greeted by a sturdy blonde aging Hilde and given a ground-floor room with twin beds and a patio all its own outside the French doors.

We didn't have to go far to meet other foreigners in Ibiza. The place was crawling with non-Spanish visitor types. Not tourists. Not yet anyway. Just errant people of all ages who dressed in colorful flowery getups and called everybody, sex-indifferent, "man." An English painter named Clifford Smith lived nearby. We came upon him on our way to town on foot in the early evening. He was walking his standard poodle whom he named Perro and spoke to in the most amusing British/Spanish accent. *Ben Ahkey, Payro* — come here, Dog — he was saying. Perro, the dog, paid Clifford no mind. He was having nothing of his master's *ben ahkey.* Clifford stood waiting for the dog to come back to him so we grabbed the moment and asked him in English where we might eat in town and if there were any popular bars we might go to. He steered us to Juanito's curbside restaurant in a tiny cobbled street close to the port. "Eat the paella, man," he advised. "And drink San Miguel beer. Skip the water."

"And a bar?" we wondered.

"La Teeyaira," he called over his shoulder as he chased and called *Ben Ahkey* louder at his dog. "Go there, man. Tell Arlene I sent you. And drink San Miguel."

As a recent hepatitis survivor, I was not allowed alcohol. So I stuck to fizzy water from a bottle at the restaurant and bar. The restaurant consisted of about ten wobbly, wooden tables set off the curb on a narrow cobbled street just off the port. The paella was passable. The owner was pleasant to us. He spoke some English. We asked about La Tierra bar. He gave it a thumbs up and pointed us in the right direction.

After dinner we moseyed over two sewer-smelling streets toward a dead-end alley to our left from whence pounded loud Beatles music from a white plaster building with a small, curved-top door in its thick wall. Down two steps and we were in a throbbing paradise. Music pounding. Wall to wall people. Everybody was foot-tapping and wriggling to the beat. But nobody danced. Apparently, La Tierra didn't have a dancing license. There were low, low tables with even lower wooden stools to sit at. One was free. We sat there. A bustling chubby woman with auburn hair, black pants and a worried look hurried over and asked, "Whaddayas want?" in Brooklynese.

She brought our drinks and asked, "Wheyuh yas from?" We told her we were American but we lived in France. "Ahm Ahlene," she shouted over the din and twisted her way back through the crowd to her bar. "Need anything — just holluh."

Arlene Kaufman owned La Tierra. She was my first Ibiza friend. She was a tough, lost, young woman of about thirty who probably needed psychiatric care but had instead opted to leave *Noo Yawk* and open a bar in Ibiza. Her boyfriend was a Scotsman named Elly who was an artist. He painted endlessly time-consuming masterpieces, then drizzled melted gold leaf over the top. He was bald. About forty-five. Smiled a lot and did the heavy lifting of beer kegs and cartons of bottles. Arlene and Elly didn't live together. He had a large studio in the old town. Arlene lived in *La Peña,* the fisherman's village with its multi-colored narrow, tall, connected houses and cobbled streets like gutters that ran right down to the sea.

I guess we had been there for about two or three days when Sue decided not to come to town with me one night. She was planning to eat a different kind of paella at a restaurant in our little suburb that was located in a sea-front building that we called The Beehive. It was a small apartment building that housed mostly foreigners. Clifford Smith lived there with Perro. Everybody, it seemed, had lived in the Beehive at some time. Even I lived there for a short while years later when I was at my most insanely unhappy. But more about that in the next volume ....

I decided not to accompany Sue Burke to her new paella spot that evening and walked into town alone to have a quick dinner at Juanito's and then hit La Tierra where the music and the crazy, wriggling people beckoned. La Tierra bar was a blessed oasis for the fun-starved, Protestant American girl I still was. So *this* was what I had been missing. How had I not heard Ray Charles singing *What I Say*? How had I missed *Can't Buy Me Love*? In a matter of days, Ibiza and its straggly foreigners, its eccentric fauna, the pigtailed ladies in black and Ibiza's morning *ensaimada* pastries and *cafes con leche* had plunked down in my lap and nuzzled me all over. I was thrilled by the smoky, noisy thundering and in love with the tuned-in young people who had been reveling behind my back. While I was still moping around up in Paris, drinking the occasional glass of hot red wine and wishing that Xavier might loosen up and come live with me in the States, the rest of the world my age was stoned.

I didn't stand at the bar that evening or even mingle with the clanking, colorful people about whom I so far understood nothing. There were no free tables. So I sat down at one across from a young man who looked American — and tired. "Is it okay if I sit here?" I said. He woke right up and beckoned me sit.

I told him my name was Susan Hoskins. He gave me his. It was Tom Wright. I drank my fizzy water slowly and gazed at the crowd. I was spellbound. Suddenly this Tom person was addressing me in a soft, mildly Southern accent. "What's a pretty girl like you doing in a place like this?" He inquired with a wry smile. I blushed and told him I was on vacation. Easter break. "I'm a teacher. In France."

As I replied to his question, I took the opportunity to eye this Tom Wright guy squarely, the way I was taught by my mom to look at people when you speak to them. Instantly, I was struck by a pair of deep brown, slightly exophthalmic eyes. Puppy eyes. Gentle eyes that lived in a large balding head. Tom Wright's smile plus those liquid brown eyes gave me pause. Here was someone very attractive who didn't look dangerous. He wore desert boots and jeans with a wrinkly t-shirt. There floated an attractive air of boyish innocence about him.

Why I mention dangerous is that I could tell that the Tierra bar was loaded with creeps. Many of the men wore flower-printed shirts of softly flowing cotton with puffy sleeves. The most flamboyant creeps wore brightly colored silk shirts — also with puffy sleeves. These shirts were often unbuttoned down the front to show off chest hairs and gold chains that didn't cost only a nickel. Those same fellows' hair was, of course, long and greasy, lank or bushy with a kinky pony tail in back. The creeps' skin was leathery. They wore bell bottoms and clanky boots with, as they were mostly on the short side, a bit of a heel.

I was later to know that the creeps in question were the dealers. It was not a good idea to get tangled up with the dealers as they frequently ended up in the very basic Ibiza jail where prisoners had to depend on their families to bring them food and money to bribe guards and buy privileges. Dealers who went to jail often depended on the girls they called their "old ladies" to provide them with what they needed. I didn't want to be anybody's "old lady."

After a couple more drinks, Tom said he would be happy to walk me back to Figueretas where he knew a painter guy called Frank Schwake, an American Sufi. Maybe we would meet up with Frank. He liked to contemplate the sea from the beach there. As we walked along, Tom told me about his family. His real dad had skipped on his mother who had then remarried a man named Keith Laumer who was a famous science fiction writer. His mom had hatched two girls with Laumer. Writers have sketchy incomes so to be sure of a steady paycheck, Keith Laumer had joined the Air Force. When Tom was a teen, the family moved to London. Keith Laumer, the writer stepfather, had been offered some kind of military/diplomatic post in England. Came time for school, Tom went to Ealing College of Art. His best friend there was Pete Townshend. Tom adored Pete's music. Pete admired Tom's photography. They had the best times together. But one day, Tom got caught with some grass and was exported out of the UK by the authorities. Hence Tom was in Ibiza — doing nothing much.

Before dropping me back at Hilde's pensión, Tom asked me to join him in a walk on the Figueretas Beach. As predicted, there was his Sufi friend Frank Schwake sitting on a rock watching the sea. Frank was about forty. He had a white-blond shock of hair which fell down over his right eye. He looked Midwestern, which he was. Iowa, I think. Being forty seemed ancient to me. "Hey man," said Tom, approaching Frank.

"How's it hangin'?" said Frank. Then silence. We sat down at Frank's side. Right away he handed Tom the joint he was smoking. Tom inhaled, coughed a bit, smiled, then handed the cigarette to me. "Thanks. But I don't smoke," I said and left it at that. I had a hunch they must be smoking marijuana. That alone gave me chills. But as they were neither drunk nor rowdy, I wasn't frightened. They were contemplative, quiet. Frank took back the joint. The guys spoke a bit then. But slowly. About Dylan. About the songs. About *North Country Girl* and *Don't think twice. It's all right.* It was Greek to me. I had never heard of Bob Dylan. But I was a girl, remember? Girls didn't do too much talking back then. We listened and absorbed men's words and their ejaculations.

Tom Wright and I became almost instantly inseparable. He was younger by five years. He was not urbane or sophisticated. But he was *cool.* With Tom, I was learning how to speak "Hippie.". For "lovely," now I said "groovy." Instead of "hello" I said "hey man." I used "far out" when I wanted to sound enthusiastic about something, and when I couldn't get my zipper zipped or find the keys I said, "What a drag!" People didn't leave a place, they "split the scene," and when you didn't know someone's girlfriend's name, you asked if that "chick" was that guy's "old lady."   Regardless of their rank in a man's life, all women were called "Baybee" by all hip men, Baybee on the street and Baybee in bed and a shrug and a mournful whining Baybeeeee in arguments they wanted to win.

We did a heap of mooning about and having sex in damp sheets in Tom's clammy room by the sea. How was the lovemaking? Abysmal. Tom, like his predecessors, was an eager pumper. As he was only twenty, his pumpings were beyond energetic and his erections popped back up almost immediately after he came. That meant we made love at the very least four or five times day — and sometimes in the night as well. I didn't mind. I loved this sweet, funny little hippie guy. He taught me hippie talk and shared his hippie life and hashish with me. I was always a sucker for learning something new. The contrast between stuffy, pulled-up Xavier Faure de la Taille and shabby jeans, cute, doe-eyed Tom Wright was proof enough I was learning something new.

I drove back and forth to Barcelona and took that creaky old Ibiza boat almost every week I had off during that summer. I was in love. So was Tom Wright. He thought the stars shone from out my eyes. He reminded me of warm salt water taffy. We walked a lot, got stoned and made love and we planned to be married the next year at Chartres Cathedral near Dreux Air Force Base where I still worked.

Hardly worth mentioning is that most of my colleagues at work thought I had gone bonkers mad. As if my queer new way of speaking and hippie getups weren't enough, I suddenly made light of everything that the Air Force base system wanted me to take seriously. I had a falling out with Lieutenant Mann, the rigid young military fellow in charge of the dorm accounts and rules. Our difference of opinion was over ladies' dress codes on base. I wore tatty jeans and tie-dyed t-shirts to work. He balked and told me to "shape up." I answered, "I do my job just as well in jeans as I would in a circle skirt." Next day, Lieutenant Mann put a note in my mailbox at the post office. "Gie us the power to see ourselves as ithers see us!" Not a direct quote from Robert Browning. But close.

Late in August in Ibiza we agreed that Tom would leave the island and come with me back to France. We would pack his gear and guitar into my little blue car and drive up to Paris together. Tom asked if his good friend Cam could come along. Cam needed to be in Paris to meet up with his parents who were flying over on holiday from Somerville, New Jersey. I agreed to take Cam along and off we went up the Route Nationale 20 to our respective new destinies. We left Barcelona at dawn. To save money and time, we had decided to share the driving and barrel right on through to Paris without stopping to sleep anywhere. I had driven most of the way and was exhausted by eight p.m. when Tom took the wheel. Cam got up front and I went to sleep in the tiny back seat of my Gordini. About twenty kilometers before Limoges, I was jolted awake by the car rolling over, then slamming into something very hard. Somehow the boys got themselves out of the front seat. For a few long seconds I was trapped and terrified in the back seat. Then I smelled gasoline, heard it dripping and came to my wits. I kicked out the back window with my Frye-booted left foot and crawled to safety. Sheer luck had it that no cars or semis came at us either way. Tom looked hangdog at me as I stood there shaking at the side of the road next to my beloved wreck of a vehicle. He shrugged and said, "Sorry, Baybeee."

I turned round and saw that we had in fact run into the stubby two-foot-tall stone barrier of an immensely high bridge spanning an immensely low ravine below. We were lucky to be alive.

As it was pitch dark night outside and we didn't know how to either get the car out of there or find ourselves a place to sleep, I went into action. I left the boys and the bridge, strode along into town and knocked on the first door I saw. It was a heavy wooden door — a château-like portal. I banged with my fists. Nobody came. I took off my boot and struck the mammoth door with the heel. Nobody came. I hollered *Au secours!* — Help! — and hit the door with my boot a second time — harder. Still nobody. It was chilly and I was scared.

Then I noticed way up high a giant brass door knocker affair which was nearly invisible, as it had gone green with age. I slammed that knocker a few times till I heard the swishing of slippered feet on gravel coming toward me. A craggy, aged man's face appeared at the door. Rheumy eyes peered at me suspiciously and with disdain. I rapidly explained what had happened. The man pulled the big door open a bit further and spent a few seconds examining my getup before caving in, casting open the heavy door and hearing me out.

The man was in his pajamas. His wife came shuffling up and bid him put on the wool bathrobe she had brought down from upstairs. "What do you want?" she asked.

I explained again. "*Bonsoir, Madame.* We had an accident on the bridge. My car is ruined and my friends are standing out in the cold on the bridge." I was nearly in tears and gasped out this last bit. "We need a hotel and a tow truck. May we use your phone?"

The woman softened and inquired, "You mean you had an automobile accident on the big bridge?"

"The car rolled over twice, then slammed into the side wall," I said. My teeth were chattering. "We all got out. But the car is ruined."

With her blue-veined hand over the big O of her mouth, she said, "There have been many accidents on that bridge. It's slippery at night when the fog rolls in. Every car that has slid on our bridge has ended up in the valley below. Nobody ever survived."

By now I was in full, open-tear-duct mode and silently sobbing. Shaking and snuffling. I wanted to crawl into the woman's arms and beg her to help us.

"Go. Hurry. Get your friends," she said in a gentle, slightly scolding mother's voice. She shooed me away with a wave. "Go. Now. I will call the tow truck.

"You can sleep here."

We did sleep there. All three in the same room between stark, white linen sheets, our heads on feather pillows. There were three beds. Madame explained the room had been her grandchildren's. "I keep their beds made up just in case. But they never come anymore. They are all grown and gone."

At eight a.m. she called us downstairs to her woody dining room and fed us a handsome breakfast of warm fresh bread and butter and three kinds of her homemade jams. Steaming hot milk was poured from a ceramic blue pitcher into our cups of strong, French country coffee. We could not stop looking at each other, amazed all three were sitting there, unscathed.

"You are lucky to be alive," said Madame. "Your car is up at the Pierre-Buffière garage. You can walk. It's not far. You can come back down here to fetch your things."

We said a hundred thank yous and set out for the garage. The mechanic said, "I fixed it so it runs. But the frame is bent. Nothing to do about that."

"Can we drive it as far as Paris?" I asked.

"Carefully," he said, handing me the keys.

I paid him and we all three got into the clown car. The whole structure was bent over. It looked like a circus car. The windows worked and the back windshield wasn't shattered and had fit right back into place. But steering was odd. The car wanted to go right when I needed it to do the opposite.

When I pulled up in front of Madame Buffière's house, I looked up to get a glimpse of its actual size. I could see that the house was hugely tall and just as deep. Then I saw it. A sign written above the door in big old-fashioned lettering across the front of the whole building. It was a faded semi-circular sign and it read:

AUBERGE DES TROIS ANGES
(THE INN OF THE THREE ANGELS)

We made it to Paris. The car was trashed. But our love affair had survived.

CHAPTER SEVENTEEN

B ecause Tom Wright's stepdad was an officer, Tom had Air Force privileges and could claim a free room in the base officers' quarters. I had my room in the women officers' building and he had his in the men's quarters. We slept back and forth almost every night. I worked. Tom took photos. We ate at the officer's club. When he grew up Tom wanted to be a famous photographer. Like Henri Cartier-Bresson or Richard Avedon. In fact, when he did finally grow up, he became the photographer for Pete Townshend's band *The Who* and many other rock groups. Our on-base arrangement worked fine till Tom got bored being stuck out in nowhere on a military base without a car and with nothing to take photos of. "I need to take pictures," he announced one day. "I'm going to live in Paris."

"Where?" I could not imagine Tom landing a flat in Paris. He had no income and hardly knew how to tie his shoes.

"At the Beat Hotel," he replied. Glib and utterly sure of himself, Tom packed up some gear, kissed me goodbye, hitched a ride to Paris and moved into the new Beat Hotel.

The *new* Beat Hotel was a very old hotel. It was located in *la rue de l'Hirondelle* just fifteen steps down from the Place St. Michel. This *new* Beat Hotel was a fleabag's fleabag. But according to lore, the original Beat Hotel in *la rue Git-le-Coeur* was worse. Its claim to fame was that William Burroughs and some other beat artist types had lived there. The nickname Beat Hotel was invented by Gregory Corso, who was a notorious beat poet junkie-about-town. When Beat Hotel number one closed, William Burroughs — the mysterious American writer and Parisian junkie-about-town — moved to the *new* Beat Hotel. The lobby was tiny, narrow and grim. The rooms papered in grimy wallpaper with dead flowers all over. Much of that paper was stained, torn or gouged. Young Tom Wright didn't mind. His friend Cam had moved in there. Cam had a motorcycle. They shared a room one flight up with someone anonymous who smoked as much dope as they did. I never saw Burroughs. He lived up top.

I went into Paris to visit Tom Wright from time to time, but despite my having plighted him my troth, the stench and the dirt and the general disarray of his digs got to me. The first day I was there, I cleaned. The second day I went out and bought gauzy white fabric to make curtains for the room. The boys were mostly supine on various beds strumming at guitars or lighting up. I sat in a chair sewing. I smoked a bit of dope myself back then. But even if I was slightly stoned, I had to DO something. I thought of myself as an industrious pothead.

It was during this hodge-podge time that the school year ended in 1964. Tom was pleased. He was convinced I would finally come live with him in that junky room in Paris. But I didn't. Rather, I wouldn't. So one fine day he got it into his head to get help. Find us a place to live. We went to call on someone he knew from Ibiza. "He's the head hipster in Paris," Tom assured me. "His name is Allan Zion. He lives in a groovy wooden pad in a garden somewhere near Montparnasse. I have his address."

We took the Métro to St. Jacques station, found *22 rue de la Tombe-Issoire*, clicked the heavy main entrance door open and entered a clean, elderly, unpretentious building of four stories. Three stairways split off the corridor to the right. But halfway down the central outdoor passage to the courtyard directly to the left was a black sliding door leading into a low-slung wooden house which was clearly not part of the main building. The house appeared to be set in a large garden. Tom rang the brass doorbell in the shape of a fish and waited. Soon a gaunt, bearded man slid back the door, stuck his head out and wondered, "Who are you? You..." he pointed at Tom, "look familiar." Then he looked me over and added, "You don't look familiar but I can handle that," and invited us into his handmade wooden pad.

Zion's house seemed to be all at ground level. The living/dining area must have covered about 350 feet square. The kitchen and bath were housed in their own nook next to the entry hallway. The living room was Zion's sleeping area with a built-in couch/bed, bookshelves and reading lamps he had apparently made himself. A stereo amplifier and turntable was within easy reach of the bed. The lampshades were large tin cans with holes drilled all over and the end cut off for the light to shine down on your book. Up two small steps was the dining area. Over top of that was an unused loft bedroom attainable by a handsome oaken staircase. Off the dining space right was a door. Zion opened it and showed us his workshop, which contained a door into the garden. Zion kept his neatly arranged tools there and had built multiple workbenches. The dining room held an extra-long wooden table with benches down either side. The table would easily have seated ten people. When I admired his table, Allan

149

Zion said, "I used to throw spaghetti parties here every Sunday night. I supplied the spaghetti. The guests brought the wine. But after a while it got to be expensive. I was feeding a crowd of freeloaders. So I started asking them to pay a couple bucks to come eat here on Sundays. Then they stopped coming. After that I started throwing my Sunday night parties without food. Guests still bring the wine. I furnish the space and the music. It wasn't long before any and everyone in Paris — hippies, doctors, diplomats, lawyers, poets, artists, models and dancers — started hearing about Zion's Sunday Nights and began flocking here. I get people from all over. I'm a legend."

I was impressed. I strolled over to the picture window which looked out onto the garden. There wasn't much greenery in that garden. Just cactus and stones and some dripping cement statues planted about. I wondered if Zion had made those statues. They were ugly so I didn't ask. There were paths made of stones and a couple of cement benches placed here and there.

Inside the garden way over to the left in the back corner against the twenty-foot-high property wall sat a cottage. A Zion-style, but way smaller, wooden house. With some added gingerbread, that little house would have suited Hansel and Gretel. I couldn't help wondering, "Is that house yours too?" I said.

Zion perked right up. "Not anymore, man. I built it. Then I sold it to this rich American guy. He can't go into the garden. He can only pass through it to get to his house. I gave him *droit de passage* which, in France, is a strict rule about passing through someone's property. You can't linger on the other person's land. Just pass through."

"So now you actually own this house and the garden?" I asked.

"Yeah. Something like that. I bought the house off two French chicks one night when they brought me home to fuck them. They had inherited it. It was just a workshop. They were asking only $600. I had that much so I bought it."

"This house for $600?" said Tom Wright. We all sat down at Zion's big table. "That's a deal."

"It was. But this place was a lot of nothing back then. It wasn't liveable. I tore most of it down. Then I re-built it all by hand. The other proprietors in the building went nuts. They live in tiny dingy apartments. They were jealous. This house, they often came knocking to insist, was not a habitation. They claimed it was to be used as what it was built for — a workshop. They said if I lived here, I needed a building permit from the city of Paris. I never applied. I just kept building. They threatened to sue me. Here in France, with an apartment building, every owner has a share in the whole property; you need unanimity among all the owners to sue someone. There are forty-three owners in this building. They don't know from unanimous. French people never can agree on anything. Besides, they are simple people. They don't even have toilets in their small apartments. They use a communal WC on the stairway landing."

"That's weird," said Tom and lit a cigarette.

I spoke up. "I am still curious about that little house you built in the back corner of the garden. How'd you get permission to do that?"

"I didn't. That had been the potting shed for the original owners of the building. They kept garden tools in there. This whole apartment building used to be owned by one family. The widow of the last proprietor still lives on the fourth floor. After her husband died, she sold it off as condominiums that they call a *co-propriété*. Now she has no more power. Everybody owns his or her own apartment. They have yearly meetings and vote on stuff. The girls I bought this place off only owned the workshop and the potting shed. Not the garden."

"So you bought the garden from the *co-propriété*?" I asked him.

"Didn't have to. The use of the garden and its maintenance belong to the person who owns the potting shed *en perpetuité*, which means forever. "I own that shed so I have the exclusive use of the garden. I'm supposed to make it pretty and maintain it. But..." Zion shrugged, lit a Gauloise and asked us why we came to see him.

Tom Wright assumed his most boyish humble air and said, "We need a place to live. Suzanne has been sick. She was living in the country. Now she's in Paris. I live at the Beat Hotel. I can't ask her to live there."

By now some of you are wondering why, at age twenty-five and half, I was actually contemplating getting married to a jobless, broke twenty-year-old hippie photographer with whom the lovemaking was thoroughly unsatisfactory. Was I crazy? In truth, I often asked myself that same question. Why would I be in love with a lover who only pumped and didn't know or care what a clitoris was? But what makes us love somebody? Why do we stick to them even if we are not completely gaga happy? It's another of life's mysteries.

Long story short, Tom Wright and I shacked up in the little cottage across the garden from Zion's house. Its owner, the famous rich American, had taken off for London for a couple of months.

At first, we got along fine living together in that tiny house. Tom would go out shooting pictures. I would shop and cook and play Little Susie Homemaker. Evenings we walked to Montparnasse and people-watched from the terrace at the Dôme café. The little house in the Tombe-Issoire was about ten city blocks from the junction of the Boulevards Raspail and Montparnasse. In those days everybody walked. Days and evenings the sidewalks were full of people out strolling with or without grocery carts, children or pets. Most times, after a meal, every French citizen took a walk with the family. Few people had television sets. And if they did, there was only one channel.

We didn't have much money. We didn't often go to movies. Sometimes there were special weekday prices at a small cinéma off the Boulevard St. Michel. Or if we felt like taking a longer walk, we'd go down to *La Cinémathèque* on the *rue d'Ulm* and take in a classic. In those days *La Cinémathèque* was Paris's only film museum. Entrance was free or nearly free. Every student, hippie and true cinéma buff queued up far ahead of screen time. If you wanted a seat, you had to get there early.

Sometimes in Montparnasse at the Café du Dome or the Café Select, we would meet up with people we knew from Ibiza. Although the Lost Generation's celebrated writers and poets were all dead and gone, Montparnasse still attracted a Bohemian set. All manner of would-be artists and writers, poets, sculptors and sundry other bull-shitters used those two cafés as their headquarters. Lots of those same folks had spent time in Ibiza, which was fast becoming *the* in place to go, hang out for cheap and find some smoke.

All nationalities gathered in Montparnasse. We mixed with Israeli spies and British dandies, Rumanian exiles and pretty Scandinavian model girls. One guy we often saw was an American painter name Peter. Peter was not a would-be painter. He painted real canvases and made his living from his work. But Peter drank. And when he drank he became violent and dangerous. He'd show up at one of the cafés at about nine p.m. and by eleven o'clock he was roaring drunk. Within seconds, he was engaged in some sort of fracas involving at least one other human being. When we went to the Montparnasse cafés, if he was there, we sat at a distance, chatting and meeting with other people who would sit down and drink with us. But we always kept one eye on Peter. If we noticed that he was getting close to sloshed, we hurriedly paid and left the premises. Peter's metamorphosis from quiet drinker to monster was so rapid, anybody might become his victim. Man or woman, Peter would zero in and decide to start beating them up. Right there in front of the whole café. He would slap a woman's face or punch some unsuspecting fellow in the jaw. Most everyone knew that when he pounced, it was up to the other men in the room or on the *terrasse* to tackle him and pull him off his prey. Often they would beat him up badly and really hurt him. His nose would bleed and/or a wound would open on his skull. But Peter didn't give up. He remained in attack mode till the waiters joined forces with those trying to control him and he would be hurled onto the sidewalk and told never to return. But a few days later he would be back. Mr. Charming. He shook hands and gave kisses at different tables and extended neutral polite greetings: *Hi. How are you? And the children? How's your work* going? *Did you get your Mobylette fixed?* Then he'd sit and drink until he became a savage again.

There were some other less-menacing characters who hung out around Montparnasse. The fauna included a couple of hack writers who concocted pornographic novels for a famous marginal publisher named Maurice Girodias. One Dutch guy banker type sat silently alone most of the time. Then once in a while, he would begin throwing chairs through windows. No reason. No provocation. He would just bust up the place. He was 86'd by the waiters and the management. But he always returned, humble and apologetic.

Occasionally his friend Cam would lend Tom Wright his Harley. Tom loved riding that huge thing, with me on the back, weaving in and out through the mad Parisian traffic and gunning the engine behind slowpoke drivers to scare them into next week. Up and down the streets and across all the bridges we would ride. It was thrilling. But I was crisp with fear. After the auto accident and the three angels' sleepover party on the way home from Ibiza, I didn't trust Tom's driving. Looking back, I realize that Tom Wright was still a kid — a post-adolescent juvenile delinquent — or almost. Did I know that? No. Of course I didn't. I was in love.

We were deliriously part of what was called the *Paris scene*. In the Sixties. Everybody was in love with everybody else and the other guy's sweetheart too. Some people lived in communes and shared their lovers as well as their food. Others got by hanging out around town cadging coins or performing scratchy violin solos outside cafés. Another way to make money in those days was to do the movie queues.

A poorly rendered guitar solo to accompany a raspy familiar Beatles tune or even an American folk song with Western movie overtones could bring in enough change for a meal. Usually the cats made the music and their old ladies passed the hat. Paris was so alive in those days. The Métro was safe until midnight. A woman alone on the street wasn't afraid she would be mugged or raped. Café life was everybody's life. On the Left Bank of Paris in those days, staying home in the evening was for invalids and sissies.

As time went by during our stay in the little house, when Tom Wright would be out shooting up Paris scenery, Allan Zion would come snooping over for a chat, a cigarette and a cup of tea. Zion smoked lots of French cigarettes. *Gauloises Bleu.* I never saw him inhale or ingest any controlled substances. But he would come out his side door, step through the garden, knock and come sit at the rustic table in the tiny house, drink his tea, smoke his *Gauloise* and tell me about how important he was on The Scene in Paris and how he was looking for the right woman — someone who was serious and had a job. "I'm tired of balling skinny model chicks," he said.

Zion was only thirty-five, but he looked older. His skin was pockmarked and yellowed from smoke. His ego, however, was in excellent fettle. The skinny had it he never smoked dope. But when he visited me in the afternoons he would rattle on as though stoned. "I play the clarinet. But music, like music is dead, man. So I took up painting. But art, man, art is like ... dead. I mean art is fucked. There is no more art. I was a sculptor for a while but sculpting is like, well, it's moribund too. So now I build things. I designed and built a pad for Memphis Slim in Montparnasse. Then I built this little house out of the tool shed. I keep pretty busy with some private stuff too. I was balling this model chick from Dior. Then I balled a skinny blonde who worked at Balenciaga. That Dior chick got jealous and freaked on me. Came and broke the big picture window over in my house."

"She did?" I had said. "How awful."

"She sneaked into the garden by night, took one of those big flagstones from the path and crashed it right through the glass. I was in bed with Ursula. The noise was deafening."

"What did you do?" I asked.

"Went back to sleep. It wasn't too cold out. We cleaned up the mess in the morning." Zion fingered his pack of Gauloises. "Those model chicks are real downers."

In Allan's company, one was but a guest on The Zion Show. He talked. About himself. Nobody else existed. I couldn't outright dislike him. I was too young to go disliking the Mr. Cool of Paris. I was impressed and awed by how many famous people he knew. I was flattered by his attentions.

Did it dawn on me that Zion was chatting me up? Nope. In fact, when Tom Wright would come in after a shooting expedition, I was eager to tell him how Zion had come to visit. I said I thought Allan very odd. But it was nice he had arranged for us to stay there, wasn't it?

It had, however, dawned on Tom Wright. One evening he began quizzing me about Zion's afternoon visits and accusing me of having slept with him while he was out taking photos. I assured him that was not true. But he hit me anyway. I swore and screamed and packed his gear and threw him and his guitar out into the garden. That was the end of Tom Wright. No more troth. No more engagement. No more wedding in Chartres Cathedral.

Was I sad? Not really. I was relieved to be alone, living in the idyllic little cottage in Zion's garden and discovering the neighborhood. I was proud. I was actually living by myself in Paris. Allan Zion did periodically try to get into my pants, but I successfully resisted and carried on inventing my life on my own.

While I was living there solo, I would often venture out at day's end and make my way around the neighborhood, drinking in the shimmery light of Paris's gloaming, the waning dusk light that still rests my eyes today. It etches the corners of roofs and outlines trees, and silhouettes the people against the twilight. I would ramble all around the 14th arrondissement where there were no buildings of more than nine stories, scads of *boulangeries* and *boucheries*, vegetable and fruit merchants, open market streets, a post office, shops, restaurants and cafés galore.

The *pièce de resistance,* of course, was Le Parc Montsouris. A mere few blocks away from the little house lived a medium-size rolling public space surrounded by a wrought iron fence painted Paris-park green. In the middle of the rear of the park was the reason for its name — Mouse Mountain. On top of a city-sized hill sat a once-glorious, Middle Eastern-style palazzo. I had always imagined that a rich aristocrat had built the manor house for his mistress who died tragically young. Then, in my illusion, the noble gentleman had bequeathed the fifteen-hectare estate to the city. Later, I found out the park had been built by Haussmann who had been ordered to build four Parisian parks by Napoleon III. For Mouse Mountain, Haussmann had concocted an English-style garden with a lake, a small waterfall, an ornate bandstand and that dollop of Moorish palazzo on top.

Le Parc Montsouris had been opened in the late nineteenth century. By 1964, the crumbling old pavilion was propped up by wooden buttresses. Still, up there it sat, majestic stone gray and turreted, its windows glinting multicolored in the sunlight. When I walked through the Parc Montsouris, I always took the left-hand path down past the *guignol* puppet show, the carousel and along the edge of the fenced-in swings and slides, halfway round the lake, past the nineteenth century bandstand. Then I would shortcut right up the steps, grab onto the cement made-to-look-like-wood rail, cross the bridge above the cascade, past the roller skating section and then walk past the back of the majestic old clapped-out mansion. Then I'd veer down to the right and take Avenue René Coty back to the little house in the garden at *22 rue de la Tombe-Issoire.* In those days, the 14th arrondissement was still authentic *vieux Paris.*

What did I do with my time when I was in the little house? Well, on Sundays, I went to Zion's parties. During the week I read books and cleaned and did laundry at the launderette. I often took long walks down to the Seine, across the many bridges to the Right Bank and into the smarmier quarters. After all, I had begun my Parisian life over there in *la rue Clément-Marot* working for Monsieur Traub near the Champs-Elysées. The office was around the corner from the Avenue Montaigne, Harry Winston, the Plaza Athenée Hotel and across the street from the elegant gray and white Christian Dior boutique. On my trips to the Right Bank, I often ventured into those hallowed places — just to sniff around and imagine myself a regular customer.

La rue St Honoré also magnetized me. The very sidewalks were redolent of subtle fragrances and all the shops oozed *chic.* Boutiques that sold perfumes sprayed their scents into the air above their shop windows. A mere walk-by was enchanting. Dreamlike. *Maybe one day,* I mused. *I can quit being a dorm counselor at the air base in Dreux and become a fashion model. Or a journalist. Or a lady of luxury living somewhere on the right bank. A grand apartment with cushy velvet couches and a button under the dining room carpet to press with my dainty foot to call the servants.* I was fantasizing. But I was also reveling in the fact that all the doors of my young life had by now been flung wide open. I was raring to pass through every single one. I had wings — and aspirations.

I hoped that maybe one day I could become a terminally elegant lady, dress in couture clothes and marry someone rich and important who would whisk me off to his country house every weekend in a Jaguar. I was twenty-five and a half. Could thirty be far behind? Mr. Underwood the Deviled Ham man's warning that day we met up in the Café Flore haunted me. He had said, *"Let me tell you something, young lady. It's okay to play house till you're twenty-five. Then you better start looking for an American guy who makes a good living."* With this in mind, I resolved that I should look for someone more dependable. A man I could take home to Mother. No more tapped-out noblemen. No more stone-broke hippies. I should find someone new and possible to date and go to bed with. Who knew? Maybe they would ask me to marry them.

In the back of my mind I sensed that my dream of a genteel Parisian life was unattainable. But my upper-crust bourgeois fantasy spurred me along anyway. I scouted for a serious man. And then I met what looked like one. A medium height, rather pudgy gentleman with rosy cheeks. He came up to me at one of Zion's Sunday night parties. As Allan Zion had said, his shindigs did not attract only members of the Bohemian expatriate set. They attracted all manner of international types on the prowl for, no doubt, some fresh hippie flesh. This portly, pinkish man that I met that evening wore a jacket and tie. He spoke to me in French. Said his name was Hubert Cornfield. "I am both American and French," he told me. "I am a movie director. I used to live in Hollywood. But I have moved back here to Paris to be close to my parents. They are getting on."

I introduced myself as Suzanne Hoskins. "I am from the States. But I live here now," I explained.

Hubert and I went out a couple of times. Dinner. Lunch. Nothing intimate. Just getting to know each other. He was indeed, just as I had thought — a gentleman. Helped me on and off with wraps and into chairs and stood up when I returned from the ladies' room.

After living in Allan's neighbor's house for a couple of months, Zion told me that the owner was expected back soon and I should find myself somewhere else to live in Paris. School would start in September and I would resume my job at the air base in Dreux, so when I had to move out of the little house, I wouldn't be homeless. But I was chagrined to have to leave that tiny chalet. I had fallen in love with living there. I think I had been happier there than perhaps ever in my life. Before I left the little house, I bought a used car. A lumbering Peugeot 403 like Célimène. Same credit. Same bank. But my new used Peugeot was gray instead of turquoise. I called her Noodles. Now that I had wheels and school was about to start again, I could drive around visiting possible new digs. From an ad in the International Herald Tribune, I found a small studio on the western outskirts of Paris near the Bois de Boulogne. It wasn't far from the road that I took to drive back and forth to the base. The studio wasn't luxurious. But it wasn't too expensive and it housed me, and the pink and green flowered curtains I had sewed up for its big windows, in relative comfort.

After a few weeks of not exactly a courtship, Hubert Cornfield suddenly invited me to come to Sunday dinner at his parents' house. I was more than just curious to accept Hubert's invitation. The senior Cornfields lived in a large ground-floor apartment in a small, elegant building on *l'Avenue des Etats-Unis* near Trocadéro. To me, that was the chic person's chic-est residential neighborhood in Paris. I was dead keen to go there. I would have the chance to wear my new pink wool — a Courrèges copy just completed the week before by Yvette, my dressmaker, in her sixth-floor walkup in the 15th arrondissement. I wore whitish pantyhose and soft pink leather *escarpins,* the "in" pumps from Carel. My dark brown hair had been perfectly coiffed into a chin-length pageboy on Saturday afternoon by Jean-Claude, Brigitte Bardot's hairdresser at Dessanges in the *Avenue Montaigne.* He had cut my bangs deep and full. The overall effect I had aimed for that fated evening was chocolate-topped *framboise bon bon.*

Hubert met me in front of the Drugstore on the Champs Elysées at about six. "You look scrumptious," he said, encircling my waist with a proprietary right arm. "Dinner at home won't be till at least eight-thirty," Hubert said. "We can take in a movie. The cinéma is right here." He made a quick gesture with his head. The movie theater *was* right there, attached to the Drugstore building. "I don't really want to go in there now," I said. "It's a lovely evening. Let's walk to your parents' house. If it's too early, we can stop for a drink at *Le Café de Paris.*"

My favorite place to preen and be seen on the *Champs Elysées* was the *Café de Paris.* The place was always filled with beautiful people to watch and possibly to impress. "Then we will arrive just in time for *apéritifs* at your parents' house," I said.

"Aristide, the butler, won't serve *aperitifs*," Hubert explained. "He claims that drinking alcohol before dinner spoils the savor of the wine."

Giving my waist a little squeeze, Hubert then pushed back my hair on one side and whispered in my ear, "Please come to the *cinéma* with me. I want to show you my cock." Hubert's suggestion ambushed my cool. "*Quoi?*" I blurted. *What?* I felt squirmy. "*Suzie, collect yourself,*" said the wee small mother in my head. I decided to continue in French. French would mean more to him. More like his *Maman* or the nanny. "Alors ... you want me to go into this *cinéma* with you so you can ... um ... show me your cock?" My voice shuddered, betraying a measure of girlish rape fear. I managed, however, to shrug a Gallic shrug and concoct a wan grin. Then, with a quick shake of my so recent *coiffure*, I returned to my schoolteacher mode and declared in English, "Don't be silly, Hubert. It's much too dark inside the *cinéma* for that."

"I have a torch," Hubert muttered, producing a small, silver flashlight from his vest pocket. It said 'Dunhill" on the side. *Oh Grandma, what a powerful flashlight you have. The better to show you my cock in a dark movie theater on the Champs-Elysées in Paris, France, with, my dear.* I arranged a tolerant, tame-the-madman smile on my lips. Then my teacher voice chimed in. "Hubert, sweetie, we are not going to the movies this evening." I put my arm through his and tugged a bit to urge him to stroll with me down the *Champs-Elysées.* "Let's just get us a lovely drink at the *Café de Paris.*"

Hubert stopped dead. He undid his arm from mine. Then, in reply to my refusal to enter a dark *cinéma* with him, his penlight and his cock, he started. On the sidewalk. On the Champs-Elysées. In the shadow of *the Arc de Triomphe*, traffic roaring up and down, passersby staring and listening. Hubert Cornfield threw a fit. In seconds, he was scarlet. "When you love somebody, you have to compromise," he seethed. "So on occasion, you do what *they* want to do." He spoke now through clenched teeth, his voice a pitch higher and louder than usual. I could tell by the way the tassels on his Italian loafers bobbled: Hubert Cornfield was hopping mad. At me! *Love?*

"I don't recall having loved you, Hubert." We had never shared more than a meal. "A dinner in a Vietnamese restaurant? A late lunch at *La Coupole?* You call *that* love?" I had never even been *near* a bed with this man and suddenly he was threatening me with both love and a loaded cock. "Look Hubert," I said. "I am delighted to have dinner at your parents'. But I don't love you and I am not going to the movies with you to look at your cock. We are walking to your parents' house. Now." Despite his now flaming red cheeks, Hubert was a good-looking, blondish, balding man. A bit pudgy yes. But sensuous. Not unappetizing. Lusty. And by now, sweating.

"You don't understand me," he whined. "This is important to me. I have a very big cock and I want you to see it." I persevered. "Not now Hubert. Some other time." I touched the sleeve of his beige chino suit jacket and rubbed it gently. I had once been a teacher. "*Allez* ..." I said. "You're not going to let one movie more or less ruin our evening, are you? After all, it's only a movie." I had pushed Hubert's loony button.

"Only a movie? Only a movie?" He roared. "Do you know who you are talking to? I am a *famous* movie director. *Movies* are my *LIFE*."

And your cock? I wondered silently. But I said, "Then go ahead. Go to the movie, Hubert." I turned and started to walk away, adding over my shoulder, "My apologies to your parents and, of course, *mes hommages* to the servants."

Emily Post would have considered it rude to renege on his parents' gracious invitation. But I, nonetheless, raced away and galloped down the Champs-Elysees, *escarpins* clopping. I was naturally disappointed not to visit Hubert's parents' splendid abode. And I was a little bit embarrassed to have disappointed his folks. Mind you, with Prince Tantrum for a son, over-endowed and under-married at thirty-six and spending their money making dud movies in Hollywood, the senior Cornfields were certainly accustomed to disappointment.

I was going on twenty-six years old. Various people's cocks were no strangers to me. In fact, I'd probably seen more men's appendages than most girls my age. The expression my parents used in hushed tones when describing my post-pubescent self was "boy crazy." That I was. Positively crazy for boys. In school, I got crushes on boys the way other girls got new hair barrettes or consumed penny candy. Back in Buffalo, I teased the boys I liked most. They returned the favor by trying to blind me with icy hard snowballs or by whipping off my stocking cap and running away with it. I admit I was more than sexually curious. I had often initiated those "Let's play doctor" games. I had enticed those innocent neighbor boys into the woods in Cazenovia Park where we showed each other our things. Now that I think of it, as I was a nervous, bookish, hysterical, sex-crazed child, France was the ideal place for me to settle.

So, in 1964 Paris, when Hubert Cornfield proposed to show me his cock, I oughtn't to have been shocked. But public displays of people's genitals, illuminated by flashlight in darkened movie theaters, was not yet part of my sexual *repertoire*. My semi-high heels ratcheted me down the Métro stairs at Franklin Roosevelt station whence I headed to the Left Bank. On that ride, I made an easy peace with the fact that, despite his wealthy parents and perfect French, Hubert Cornfield was not the man for me.

In any case, in order to escape Hubert and a private viewing of his cock by flashlight and even a possible marriage proposal from his parents, I bee-lined it straight to *22 rue de la Tombe-Issoire* and Allan Zion's funky hippie Sunday soirée. When I changed trains at *Trocadéro* and headed toward *Nation via Denfert-Rochereau,* something told me that my wide-eyed dreams of an elegant bourgeois Right Bank life were on the wane. Not yet dead. But fast fading.

Allan Zion was a curious fellow. He claimed to have been living on the GI Bill in Paris since the War. Now that he is no longer around to protest, I dared call his attention to the fact that he was born in 1930. The War ended in '45. Zion would have then been fifteen and in high school in Massachusetts. Other than using wartime ration coupons when he biked to the store for his mom, no inconvenience from World War II had so much as grazed his life. His French, however, was suspiciously excellent. On Sunday nights, there were always shiny black cars with diplomatic license plates parked every which way outside his modest apartment building. Did Zion have a private income? I always wondered, did Allan Zion work for the CIA?

When I arrived at Zion's wooden house in the old stone building's courtyard that evening, I was still dressed to the teeth and coiffed to the nines. I rang the brass fish doorbell. Zion greeted me with a hearty *Bonsoir*, a kiss on each cheek and a grope about my short pink skirt. The grope was anything but a hug. So be it. I was cute. Zion was famously horny.

The Beatles were pounding out *Can't Buy Me Love.* I was too well-dressed to dance. So I had perched in the main room on the edge of

Zion's couch/bed, I was chatting to someone seated to my right. A man. I was laughing hard so maybe it was Mason Hoffenberg. Yes. It was Mason. Now I recall. Mason had a gift. He could make the world laugh. That evening he held a flapping moth in his open palm. "I'd like you meet my pet moth," he told me, showing me this pathetic spotted, wingèd creature whose worried feet he held firmly between yellowed fingers. I was not as flummoxed by Mason's pet moth as I had been by Hubert's earlier proposition, but I was not about to ask if I could hold it.

"Oh, funny," I said. "A pet moth is a funny idea." And I meant it. "His name is Rapaport," Mason explained, without cracking a smile.

Mason Hoffenberg was a writer. He also took drugs. He wrote the cult porn novel *Candy* with his crony Terry Southern. Need I remind you again? It was the Sixties. People were committed to the absurd. Mason's pet moth idea did not seem all that odd. Pet moths. People with third-eye holes drilled in their foreheads. Naked babies left in freezing *Strawberry Fields* overnight by acid-addled parents. Men dressed in flowing turquoise gowns spattered with rhinestones wearing tiaras and pushing off from the curb on thunderous Harley Davidsons. Nothing surprised any of us much. Signs of the times.

Just as I was about to get up and seek more salubrious company, a silky man's voice from above my head said, "Well, well, well and who is this pretty girl in the pink dress?" I looked up and saw a youngish, handsome, older blond man standing there with a heavy laptop-sized UHER tape recorder slung around him on a strap. He was holding a microphone. I knew who he was. He was the rich owner of the little wooden house across the garden where I had just lived for two months. He looked very different from what I had imagined. He wore faded jeans and a rumpled plaid shirt with the sleeves rolled up. His unruly sandy-colored hair stood up all over his head. He wasn't unattractive. Just *négligé*. He did not look rich. But he did look sophisticated and worldly. "Say something," he said and thrust the microphone toward my face.

"I see you're back from London," I said.

CHAPTER EIGHTEEN

A lthough their names were eerily similar, I could never have confused stocky, balding, standard issue Tom *Wright*, the hippie, with Tom *White*, the well-spoken, curly-haired sophisticate with the tape recorder slung around his middle. White was tall, thin, tan and dishy. I stood right up and engaged him in conversation.

While I was living in his house, Allan Zion had told me few things about Tom White. He was American. Heir to a large fortune. He hailed from Santa Barbara, California. He was thirty-four, married. His wife, Veronika, a dark-haired Liz Taylor lookalike actress, was German-American. Just that year, Veronika had left Tom White for a Guinness and moved to London. According to Zion, Veronika's Guinness was a gay Guinness. But she didn't much mind either way. After all, a Guinness was a Guinness. Not that I knew what that meant. But it sounded so jet set that I was all ears anyway.

Veronika, Zion told me, now lived in a sprawling London flat in Barkston Gardens, a swanky address where both ceilings and rents were highest. After she had gone, Tom gave up their elegant apartment in *la rue de Passy* and shifted to the more Bohemian Left Bank. The tiny house in *la rue de la Tombe-Issoire* wasn't legal. But that didn't stop Allan Zion from selling it to Tom White who didn't seem to care. "He just gave me the $15,000 cash," said Allan. "He has too much money. He never worked a day in his life. He's a fuckin' playboy," he added with a snoot of disdain.

I remembered that Allan had told me the little house — not his larger house — came with the forever exclusive right to enter, use and maintain the garden. So I asked him about it. "Did you have to give up your rights to the garden when you sold the cottage to Tom White?"

"Oh no," said Allan. "I made him write me a letter saying he renounced those rights and turned them over to me. I told you. He only has a right of passage through the garden to get to his house."

When I encountered him that first evening at Zion's, Tom White had indeed just returned from England. We struck up a casual conversation. I asked about why he went to London. He told me he had gone there to take his wife, Veronika, some money for her pelmets.

"What exactly are pelmets?" I asked then. We were standing near the kitchen. The music was loud. We had to shout.

Tom explained that pelmets were part of a lavish curtain contraption, at that time more or less native to the British Isles. "Pelmets," Tom hollered above the party's din, "conceal the unsightly rods and strings which operate the drapes. They are like a cornice or a valance. Pelmets are usually upholstered. In London, they have to be custom made. Veronika says they are the most expensive part of one's draperies. That's why I had to take her the ten thousand dollars. To cover the cost of her curtain covers." He laughed at his own pun here and lit a cigarette.

Suddenly, from across the room, Zion called out my name. "Suzanne!" He cried. "You're wanted on the phone."

I had so recently moved out of the little house that my phone number was still the same as Zion's. Phone installation in Paris in the Sixties took at least one year and usually involved some sort of under-the-table donation to the post office chap who kept the list of applicants. To avoid Tom having to wait for a phone when he moved into the little house, Zion had rigged something so he and Tom White could share the line.

"Suzanne!" Allan's voice rang out from across the house again, "You're wanted on the phone." I scampered across the room and grabbed the receiver off the table. "*Allo?*"

"Suzanne! It's Hubert. I am coming to fetch you. We need to talk," he said.

It was Sunday night. Hubert knew where he might find me. *Gulp.* "I just dropped in over here," I said. "I'm going right home. I'm not feeling well."

"I'll drive you home," Hubert insisted. "I'm still at my parents'. Stay right there. I can be at Zion's in twenty minutes."

I hung up in a panic. The last thing I wanted to do was to be shown his cock and possibly mauled by Hubert Cornfield in the lavish, leathery comfort of his silver gray Lancia. I raced back to Tom White's side, tugged at his sleeve and said, "What are you doing for dinner?"

Tom White flashed me a bemused grin. "Are you inviting me to dinner?" he asked.

"Yes. I am famished. Can we go right now?"

"What kind of food do you like to eat?" Tom asked.

"Anything. I haven't eaten all day." I threw him my best waif look. "Please ..." I pulled at the strap on his tape recorder. "Let's go now."

"I have to put my dog Chico inside the house and stash the tape recorder," said Tom. "I'll meet you outside in two minutes. Mine is the Bentley. It's parked next to the church."

I dug my elegant gray wool coat with the pleated skirt out from under a heap of wraps and ponchos at the back of Allan's bed/couch. I shook my coat to remove any lingering flower child cooties and donned it in seconds.

"You leaving so soon?" I heard Allan's voice call out from across the room.

"I'm not feeling well," I said. "I have to go home now. I'll call you during the week."

I hustled myself down Zion's exit passage out into the building corridor, then beelined it out the door into the street. Looking both ways for signs of Hubert's impending Lancia, I ducked into *La Villa St. Jacques,* the side alley where the imposing metallic gray and black Bentley was parked. I crept behind the car and stood there, concealed by its massive body. *How strange,* I mused. All the time I lived here in the little house, I had been wondering who owned this huge car. That type of elegant car didn't jibe with the artsy, working class neighborhood. Yet it had been parked there every day of my sojourn in Tom White's little house. Of course it had. He was in London.

"Suzanne?" I heard Tom's silver spoon accent exclaim. "Is that you skulking about behind my car?"

I started to giggle. *Did I look like a fugitive?* He came around and opened the passenger side door. "Get in," he said with a grin. "You'll be better able to hide in there."

As I settled myself and my coat's wide skirt into the front seat of that cushy big car, I noticed I had butterflies. Not the love variety. Not yet. These butterflies were of adventure born. I could feel it. I was on the verge of escaping the mundane life of an average, expatriate, schoolteacher girl who had only fleetingly ever dared imagine herself heading out to dinner in Paris with a rich, hippie playboy in a Bentley Silver Cloud.

When we got to La Coupole, the obsequious head waiter shook Tom's hand and seated us where he liked to be placed on a center *banquette* facing the gigantic bouquet of fresh flowers that always graced the middle of that fabled dining room. We were on the bistro side where the hip people sat. The other side — on the right as you walked in — was reserved for the *bourgeois*. The menu was the same on both sides. The prices too. But some people preferred linen to paper tablecloths.

All I could think of then was how angry Hubert would be when he got to Zion's and found me gone. What would he say? Or do? He was so volatile. He might do something rash like push Allan or pick a quarrel with some crazed druggie.

"You seem preoccupied," said Tom White. "Is something wrong?"

I couldn't help it. I spilled the beans. "I'm on the lam from Hubert Cornfield," I said. "He's after me."

"I'm sure he's not the only one," said Tom. "You're a very pretty girl."

"Thank you," I said and blushed. "That phone call at Zion's was from Hubert. He was coming to get me at Allan's. As we were leaving, his car pulled in right behind us when you pulled out."

"Oh ho," said Tom. "That's why you were crouching behind the Bentley." He laughed and added. "Before I went to London and let Allan stash you in my house, he didn't tell me how pretty you are."

"I wasn't crouching," I said. "I was lurking."

"Oh yes," he nodded. "You were definitely lurking."

Tom picked up the menu then and suggested, "Why don't you have the lamb curry? It's the best in Paris," he recommended. "And a nice big glass of Guinness. Guinness is good for you." Tom smiled and said. "You know those ads?"

"Not really," I said.

"In England all the billboards advertise Guinness with that slogan: 'Guinness is Good For You.' I thought you might have heard of that."

"I've never tasted Guinness. Is it beer? Is it really good for me?" I asked him.

"It's a kind of beer. Yes. See if you like it. If not, you can spit it out," he laughed and motioned for the waiter. Tom ordered the same thing for us both in passably good, prep school French and then said, "I hope Zion didn't see us leaving together."

"Why?" I wondered through a chew of crunchy baguette.

"Because he is hot for your bod, young lady," said Tom. "And old man Zion does not appreciate competition."

"Allan?" I said. "He doesn't stand a chance with me. While you were away he tried to seduce me a few times. But he's not my type." Just then my large, blackish Guinness came topped with a froth of milk chocolate-colored foam. I sipped at it. Then set down the big stemmed glass. "Mm, tangy," I said and threw Tom a sideways look, laced with my own special brand of *coquetterie*. "Zion can fight it out with Hubert Cornfield then." I chuckled. "Anyway, I lied. I told them both I wasn't feeling well and was going straight home."

"Phew!" said Tom with a conspiratorial wink. "It's better they don't know you're with me."

When we got back to the building in *la rue de la Tombe-Issoire* after dinner and headed down the passage, Zion's house was dark. The black shade was down on the big picture window that faced the garden. Tom whispered. "He usually closes up shop at ten, or latest, ten-thirty. French law says you can't make noise in a building after ten p.m. As he has these parties every Sunday and every one of the forty-three neighbors in this four-story apartment building above the garden has called the cops at least once, Allan is more and more cautious about obeying the law."

It was true. Every Sunday at ten p.m., Allan would begin circulating through the crowd crying, *"La boutique ferme. On ferme la boutique!"* in his impeccable French. Then he would double back and start again in English, "Closing time. We're closing now. Get your coats. Time to go home." He would traipse through the garden, voice the same messages and clear out the rabble. By eleven, he would be in bed.

Before we entered the building, Tom had advised that we tiptoe in through the metal gate in the middle of the garden fence. "Pray it doesn't squeak," he said. "And keep quiet."

The way the two garden houses faced each other, Zion could see any and everything Tom White got up to outside his little house. But once inside, Zion could only guess at who Tom might have brought home that night.

It's not difficult to remember how I felt after that first dinner with Tom White at La Coupole. The word dazzled comes to mind. The compliments, the measured speech, the complicit jokes and finally — the little house — the very co-incidence of that sweet little house belonging to the first and only Prince Charming I had ever met in my whole almost twenty-six years of life.

Yes. I was dazzled.

After living in it for two months, stitching up curtains for the windows that I had cleaned, and supplying it with a discarded armchair I had found on the street, I was smitten with that little house and its singular Left Bank location.

And now I had met my own very own 14th arrondissement connection. Tom White — the one person who might possibly cement my attachment to this spot on the French earth where I felt so *me*.

It must have been midnight when we got safely and discreetly back into the little house. Once inside, without much preamble, Tom White took me in his arms. First he kissed me gently and then a bit less so. *Should I resist?* I only thought that for seconds because what I really wanted to do was kiss him back. I opened my mouth. He simultaneously thrust his smoky tongue into my mouth and ran his hand smoothly up under my pink skirt and down into my undies. Once inside my lace panties, he caressed my pussy, first softly and then with some pressure. He asked me, "Do you like this?" I swooned and sighed and whispered *yes*. His hand was right where I needed it to be. On the outer skin of the very spot where my hungry clitoris lived. The mounting excitement was almost too much. It threw my mind into a jumble. Here I was with a handsome, debonair, rich, American playboy who was touching me in the one place most men never had. I swelled and Tom pressed and rubbed a bit harder. I pressed my body against him and felt his erection hard and strong. I remember being thrilled. The kind of thrilled where small angel wings run up and down your arms and legs. And speaking of legs, mine were trembling. I was shaking. I was being made love to by Mr. Right who was not Mr. Wright but rather Mr. White. The jumble in my head gave way to passion.

"Shall we go upstairs?" Tom said.

I followed him up the rickety wooden steps. He took off my clothes. Not roughly or with haste. Slowly, he unzipped the back of my dress and cast it to the floor. There was a tiny light on the bookshelf over the bed. Music was playing. Indian music. "Do you like ragas?" Tom inquired, stroking my breasts.

Ragas, Guinness, pelmets. It was all news to me. "Sounds nice," I said as I wriggled out of my panty hose and sat there in my undies, waiting for a sign.

Tom White just stared at me. "You are really so pretty," he said. "It was not immediately obvious when I met you. But now..."

"Now what?" I asked.

He reached over and brushed his palms across my breasts. "You have such sweet small breasts," he said. "I love the way you are. Long and lean and not quite perfect. And ..." he took my shoulder and tipped me slightly sideways for a better look. "You're really all over pretty."

"How pretty?" I laughed. "Just how pretty am I?"

"Top two percent," he told me. "Easily top two percent." Then he moved his hand down my torso till he reached my undies and said, "These things are against the rules."

"What things?"

He didn't answer. Just slid off my undies without a word. "Those!" he said and threw them to the floor.

Once we had removed all my clothes, Tom took off his shirt and jeans and threw them to the floor as well. He wore no underwear. No socks either. But that no longer mattered as we were both naked now, breathing like two freight trains and sliding sweaty all over each other.

Before attempting to penetrate me immediately — the way other men I had slithered about with always did — Tom White moved his head down my body, kissing all the way, to my fluffy parts. He opened the lips with one hand and placed his wet mouth on my clit.

I almost died. I thought I had vast sexual experience. But I was wrong. Nobody had ever done this to me before. Tom sucked and licked and lapped at me the way a cat drinks milk. And just when I was sufficiently swollen and gasping, he slid his lithe, tan body back up mine, entered me ever so slowly, keeping his right hand firmly inside my pussy. He stroked my tumid clitoris. Pumped in and out as my body tensed and then relaxed then tensed again. It was magic. He knew how clitorises liked to be touched. He could not only locate one, he knew exactly what to do with it. He pumped. Yes, he did pump. He was a guy. With a penis. But all the while he kept his hand moving rhythmically against my clit and when he came so did I.

I suppose even if Tom White had been Godzilla, the idea of making love in the little house with its jet-setter owner would have enraptured me. Nonetheless, I was more than utterly charmed and, of all things, sexually satisfied. Afterward, Tom smoked. We talked. He told me his father had been a famous violinist. I told him mine was a butcher who had turned to business. He said his father had divorced his mother when he and his brother, David, were still very small. Our time passed in a friendly, sharing way. I told Tom that my parents were still together but that my mother was not well. "My father died when I was twelve," he said. I winced. "And your mother? Where is she now?"

"She's somewhere in a loony bin or living with some nice people who can stand her. She abandoned us when my father threw her out. I didn't see her much when I was a child."

"Can you see her now?" I wondered.

"I don't want to. She's suing me. For money. She knows I inherited and she wants a monthly stipend."

"Will you give it to her?" I said, half asleep.

"No I will not. She never took care of me. She never did anything for me. Why would I give her money?"

"Because she's your mother," I said, "I mean, is it a lot of money?"

"She wants sixty-five dollars a month. It's not on. My brother David and I agreed. We do not give her a cent." Tom said, about to light another cigarette.

I looked at the clock on the shelf. It read two-forty-five a.m. "I have to go to sleep now," I said.

Tom look surprised. But he didn't resist. He lay down beside me and curled his arm under my neck. I went quickly off to sleep, snuggled close to my handsome new lover. Fifteen minutes later I was abruptly awakened by the noise of a cat frantically scratching at the window to get in. He or she was screech meowing for all the neighbors to hear.

Tom sat right up and got to his naked feet to open the small window on the side of the bedroom. But before he unhooked the latch, he said to me, "Hold Chico! Hold the dog. He doesn't like the cat."

I am no good with animals. Never was. To my chagrin, I have never had or wanted to have a pet. So Tom's urgent command of "Hold Chico!" was asking a bit much. I had no clue how to hold a fuzzy big dog down while an angry cat is let into a very small room.

I sat up and called the dog to me. As he didn't know me, he didn't waggle up to my side and let me hold him. He cowered. The room was minuscule so I reached toward the far wall, tried to grab the dog's collar and missed.

Tom somehow had confidence in my veterinary talents because without looking my way to see if indeed I had hold of the dog, he let in the cat.

A noisy, whirlwind dog and cat fight ensued. I was petrified — plastered naked and shaking against the wall. In the semi-dark room, it looked like one of those cartoons where you just see whizzing circles of fluff and eyeballs and tails.

That was the first time I had ever witnessed such a fracas. It was also the first time I had observed Tom White at his ablest best. Later on, I came to call this ordinarily absent persona of his Mr. Emergency.

In an attempt to prevent an assassination, Tom grabbed at the animals in mid-flight. The first one he caught was the cat. That cat made a noise you would only recognize from a horror movie. Then, she promptly bit a great hole in Tom's wrist, piercing an artery which unleashed a terrific spurting of blood. The window was still wide open. Tom hurled the cat back out onto to the roof of the adjoining shed and said, "Suzanne, get my belt."

I was better equipped to get a belt than to hold a dog. I yanked the belt out of his jeans and started to fashion a tourniquet on his arm. The blood didn't flow. It squirted. However, he turned his hand and whenever I tried to block the flow by drawing the belt tighter, it still wasn't working. The blood just kept spurting and squirting out in wide arcs, inundating the bed and me, soaking the dog and streaking red my Prince Charming's tanned, nude chest.

"Call Zion!" he said.

"Huh?" I had to shake my head. Was he serious?

"Go get Zion," he ordered.

"But ..." I started. I snatched a pillowcase off the pillow and wrapped Tom's arm in that. "Hold your arm up," I said.

He held the belt tight and his arm higher, but the blood kept coming. In seconds, the pillowcase was wet and red. Tom said again, "Suzanne, go get Allan."

Enter a quandary. I stopped cold and thought about how desperately

I did not want Zion to know that I was in Tom White's bed. Seconds later, I grabbed my senses and recovered my rumpled pink dress from the floor, slid barefoot into my *escarpins* and started more or less sliding sideways, back against the wall, down the slippery wooden stairs to get help. Any old help would be better than losing the one man in the history of what the French call my *vie de femme* who had bothered to give me an orgasm. I liked orgasms. And I liked this man and I liked his house and his car and I even liked the way he smelled. I couldn't very well just let my first and only Prince Charming expire before my eyes. Maybe if I hadn't got Zion to drive us to the hospital at three a.m on that cold November night, I would never have been telling you the story of *La rue de la Sombre Histoire*. But I did get help. And I will tell you that story.

The ensuing minutes went something like this: Knock knock! "Allan! It's Suzanne." A whispering shout.

Nothing.

Knock knock knock knock! Pound pound pound. "Allan! Get up! Tom is bleeding. Get up!" A normal-voiced holler.

"Mmmmrrrfff," gurgled a voice from within.

Bam bam bam bam with the flat of my hand. I kicked the door a few times and shouted, "Allan, it's me. Suzanne. Please get up and help us. Tom is bleeding to death." This last was a very loud yell. I thought about the neighbors.

Finally, finally the door opened and Zion, stark naked, said blearily, "What are *you* doing here?"

What *was* I doing there? Why was I standing, shivering in my pink dress minus my underpants in a Parisian hippie's garden at three a.m?

"It's Tom," I managed. "He's bleeding."

"Tom White?" said Allan.

"Yes. Tom. Next door. The cat bit him in the arm. Hit an artery. Blood's squirting everywhere." My teeth chattered. "He says you have to drive us to l'Hôpital Cochin."

"Come on in," he grumbled. Allan opened the wooden door wider and shivered his skinny bum back into his house. I followed, "We have to hurry. He's losing a lot of blood," and kept talking. "Is your car right outside?"

"L'Hôpital Cochin is only two blocks from here," Allan muttered as

172

he dragged on his jeans. "And he wants a *ride?*" Zion didn't approve of Tom White. Or, needless to say, of my presence as the jolly pink messenger who had so obviously been recently naked with his smarmy neighbor. He gave a harrumph as he buttoned up his blue work shirt. "Next thing we know, he'll want a fucking fur-lined toilet seat."

The intern on duty stopped the bleeding, cleaned and bandaged the wound, gave Tom a tetanus shot and told him not to eat pork for eight days. Zion drove us wordlessly back to the house and dropped us at his door. I went ahead, opened the garden gate and started down the path to the little house. From behind me, Tom whispered, "Zion is really pissed off."

"Well, I did wake him up at three o'clock in the morning," I said as I opened the little house door with Tom's key.

"I know his face," said Tom. "It goes yellower. He was furious." Tom shed his clothes and headed back up the stairs to bed. I did likewise. The bloodied sheets had dried.

"Have you got any clean sheets?" I asked Tom.

In bed, sitting up, Tom lit a cigarette and passed it to me with his bandaged hand. "Laundry. I took 'em yesterday. These'll be a little scratchy. But it's all we have," he said.

I put up my palm to indicate *no thanks* about the cigarette.

"You don't smoke?" he asked.

"Never did," I said. "Not even in high school."

"Everybody smokes," said Tom, handing me the menthol cigarette anyway.

I took the cigarette, inhaled and coughed. Tears ran down my cheeks. I was choking. *My turn to die in this bed*, I thought. Tom quickly relieved me of the cigarette, stubbed it out and said, "You okay?"

"I'll live," I said, chuckling.

"Let's go to back sleep the way we were before," he said. "I liked how you snuggled me. The women I fuck aren't snugglers. They usually get dressed and go home right away. You stayed."

"I like you," I said. "Maybe I even love you a little," I said with a grin.

"That would be so nice," Tom replied. "I haven't heard that love word pronounced in reference to me in many a year." He put out his cigarette, reached over and lay me down gently, as though I was made of porcelain. Then he lay himself down beside me and said, "Snuggle me again, please."

I nestled down next to him. He felt like a tall, boney little boy. He collapsed against me. "Thanks," he said, then whispered, "Can I call you Snuggy?"

"Sure," I said, and tucked myself in closer.

As it turned out, I was in love. And so was he. It had happened. I had finally met a white American man I could take home to my mother, a man who was articulate and kind, funny, handsome and rich. A man who knew how to make me come and who had asked me to snuggle him. I was ecstatic. I just knew I would know how to give that dear man all the tender affection he had never gotten from his mother. His job? To rescue me from the humdrum world of the American Air Force base at Dreux. Whenever I wasn't working, we hung out together. It felt like the perfect match. And, best of all, every bit of it happened in that little house in the garden in the 14th arrondissement.

I sure hoped Marguerite Ratier would approve.

EPILOGUE

1 964 was the very beginning of *La Sombre Histoire*, a dark story. Since then, I have often had occasion to wonder what gust of ill wind blew me into that preposterous venue? Of course, I had fallen in love. True love might have been enough to carry me through the rest of my life. But it wasn't.

Maybe I jumped in too soon. I had always been enthusiastic. I loved taking risks. But when I took up with Prince Charming, I should have remembered my Nanny Hoskins warning to me in my high chair aged two, "Suzie. Soups's hot. Don't touch." I had instantly plunged my pudgy pink hand into Nanny's red-hot soup. Then I'd screamed bloody murder till they scooped me up and ran my scalded patty under the cold water tap. As that hand grew slimmer and whiter and older, I continued to take blind risks. Life was a hot potato that I juggled recklessly. Sometimes I fumbled. And suffered ridicule or came to harm. As time went along, my entire existence became peppered with scrapes, littered with dead dreams and star-crossed by the vagaries of astrology. But there was nobody anymore to yank me from my high chair, race me into the kitchen and run me under cold water. I had to learn to do that myself.

 SUZANNE WHITE lives in Provence. She
is writing the second volume of her autobiography - Umitigated Gaul
–A Lifetime in France.

Made in the USA
Middletown, DE
14 July 2017